The FALL & RISE of British Railways STEAM

Peter Townsend & John Stretton

The
FALL & RISE
of
British Railways
STEAM

Peter Townsend & John Stretton

RAILWAY HERITAGE
from
The NOSTALGIA Collection

First published in 2010

British Library Cataloguing in Publication Data

A catalogue record for this book is available from the British Library.

ISBN 978 1 85794 330 6

Silver Link Publishing Ltd
The Trundle
Ringstead Road
Great Addington
Kettering
Northants NN14 4BW

Tel/Fax: 01536 330588
email: sales@nostalgiacollection.com
Website: www.nostalgiacollection.com

Printed and bound in the Czech Republic

Please note:
Silver Link Publishing Ltd (Silver Link) is not responsible for the content of external websites. The reasons for this are as follows:
• Silver Link does not produce them or maintain/up date them and cannot change them.
• Such sites can be changed without Silver Link's knowledge or agreement.

Where external links are given they may be to websites which also offer commercial services, such as online purchasing. The inclusion of a link or links to a website(s) in our books should not be taken or understood to be an endorsement of any kind of that website(s) or the site's owners, their products or services.

Frontispiece:
Top: Before — epitomising the everyday view when steam was King, 'Royal Scot' No 46115 *Scots Guardsman* steams through Macclesfield on 6 June 1953 with a WCML express. The lamp standard, semaphore signals, telegraph pole and the fireman resting on the cabside between shovelling duties are all redolent of the period. *E. R. Morten, MJS collection*

Bottom: After — thankfully all has not been lost and many steam locomotives have been saved from oxyacetylene and have been preserved. Despite the doom-mongers who said that a good number of those saved would never run again, and certainly not on the main line, the passing years have seen an increasing collection of types that have proved everyone wrong! One such is that same *Scots Guardsman*, now restored to rude health and, looking as good as it ever did in BR days, is seen here on 7 February 2009, with an appropriate 'Thames-Clyde Express' headboard, running on the Settle-Carlisle line, on the southern approach to Horton-in-Ribblesdale station. *David Richards*

Title Page:
Bordon Stretching out its existence while temporarily between duties, Class 'U' No 31639, in fine external condition, is captured at Bordon, east Hampshire, at the end of the short ex-LSWR branch from Bentley, on 9 January 1966. Built in May 1931 with

right-hand drive, and a well-travelled loco, it is here shedded at Guildford, from where it was withdrawn on 27 June 1966 after a 2½-year stint there. The branch closed on 4 April 1966 and the loco was cut at Cashmore s yard in Newport in September of that year. *MJS collection*

Above: **Redhill** A graphic picture of why the main-line steam railway was not always an attractive place to work! On 8 January 1963, with that winter's snow still very much in situ, a member of Redhill shed's staff trudges over the tracks with a wheelbarrow stuffed with supplies for the sand furnace. His body language says it all, with hunched shoulders and a resigned look on his face! *Ray Ruffell, Silver Link collection*

Acknowledgements

Such was the response to and gratifying success of your authors' previous magnum opus – *The Last Years of BR STEAM 1965-68* – that we have been asked to produce a sort of follow-up volume. Not believing that a 'Volume 2' would be appropriate, we have instead embarked on tracing the 'fall and rise' of the steam engine on the UK's main line tracks from 1955 to date. There has been much midnight oil burned by your two compilers – and not a little grief, heartache and frustration along the way(!) – but they have been assisted by many willing helpers. As with any project, it is the personages in the background that have oiled wheels, coaled tenders and tapped rails to ensure that the project stayed on course

Many of the illustrations have come from our own resources, but there are so many, without whom... The following people/organisations (in no particular order) are due our thanks and gratitude: the many photographers who have been ready to loan their material and who are credited where appropriate, various books and magazines, www.sixbellsjunction.co.uk, Frances Townsend, Brian Morrison, Mike McManus' series of books on BR Stock Changes & Withdrawal Dates, Roger Butcher and his knowledge and enthusiasm for the scrap years, Cliff Thomas, Alex Hall, Jim Gosney, Richard Wells and David Richards. Thanks are also due to Will Adams of Keyword Ltd for his text editing.

They have all played their part, some with more realisation than others (!) and we are both extremely grateful to them. If any feel their contribution has been less than they had hoped, they can be assured it is purely due to space constraints.

Despite the demands of this project, not least in time, shoe-horning it between other commitments, your authors have derived much pleasure along the way. We hope that you, the reader, will also enjoy the fruits of our labours and, in no less a way, appreciate our time and effort in attempting to bring you an exciting, entertaining, instructive and fulfilling product. Any errors are ours entirely and we beg forgiveness if you spot any! Any corrections, comments and/or suggestions will be gladly received c/o the publisher's address.

We both thought we knew much of the story, having lived through it, but both of us have learned so much in our work on this book and we hope we may have also increased your knowledge in one or two things.

John Stretton, Gloucestershire
Peter Townsend, Northamptonshire

Contents

BRITISH RAILWAYS BOARD (M)   BR 4405

C 99918

LLANFAIRPWLLGWYNGYLLGOGERYCHWYRNDROBWLLLLANTYSILIOGOGOGOCH

PLATFORM TICKET 3d.

AVAILABLE ONE HOUR ON DAY OF ISSUE ONLY
NOT VALID IN TRAINS. NOT TRANSFERABLE.

FOR CONDITIONS SEE OVER

| 1 | 2 | 3 | 4 | 5 | 6 | 7 | 8 | 9 | 10 | 11 | 12 |

C 99918

Introduction

Following the publication of the 1955 Modernisation Plan, which set out to establish the future of Britain's rail network, the writing was, it seemed, on the wall for steam traction. The decline at first was slow, but following the further much revised plans revealed in *The Reshaping of British Railways* - two reports published in the early 1960s and commonly referred to as the Beeching Report - the pace of change gathered speed. The move to diesel and electric traction was further hastened by the considerable contraction of the network as branch lines closed the length and breadth of the country.

The last steam locomotive built for British Railways, aptly named *Evening Star*, was outshopped from Swindon Works in 1960 and amazingly the last steam locomotives were withdrawn from service in August 1968!

This decline forms the first part of our study - The Fall. We take a region-by-region look at steam at work from 1955 through to 1968 on branch lines and main lines, on passenger turns and on freight duties. We see these mighty giants of steam on shed, at rest and at speed - we catch glimpses of the people involved from cleaners through to top link drivers. These were halcyon days for those old enough to recall them - steam dominated the early years and there was a pride in evidence as many locos were still outshopped or maintained in gleaming glory! Sadly, as 1968 approached ever more rapidly, gleaming glory turned into dirty dilapidation! Hundreds upon hundreds of locomotives were sent to the breakers' yards to be cut up and turned into scrap.

This forms the second section of our study - 'The Scrapyard Years'. As the modernisation gathered pace the number of locations and companies involved in the wholesale slaughter rose rapidly and we take a look at a representative number of locations - the 'abattoirs of steam' are not places for enthusiasts to dwell too long and indeed the vast majority of locomotives were despatched by the cutter's torch all too rapidly, and within a short period of time the yards had either disappeared altogether or had moved on to other work. However, amongst the scenes of devastation and enthusiasts' despair there was something remarkable happening. Hardly noticeable at first, as it seemed like all the rest, but then as a trickle became a flood one yard began expanding; again at first it seemed that this was simply inevitable as the cutter's torch could not cope with the deluge! Then enthusiasts began noticing that wagons were being cut up at this yard but locomotives were not - this was the remarkable Dai Woodham's yard at Barry Docks in South Wales. Locomotives were going to Dai but not to die! Thanks in large part to this remarkable man we are able to move to...

Our third section - The Rise. This is where we marvel at what has been achieved in the years since 1968. We look at the early years when the first locomotives were being first reserved, then purchased (often gradually) and eventually moved from the yards at Barry to locations all over the country. The early locations were often fledgling preserved lines - where groups of enthusiasts had got together and decided they would save or reopen a branch line!

The impossible dream often turned out to be just that! Slowly but surely, however, schemes began to take root, while at the same time locomotive wheels began to turn again. Eventually short stretches of line were reopened - yards soon turned into miles and one station into two, three and four or more! Having been banned seemingly for ever, we see how steam returned to the main line; once again the giants of steam could flex their power and to the enjoyment of thousands be seen once again out there in the wild!

We conclude in fine style with a look at the thriving steam scene we have today - a real success story with over 8 million visitors a year to preserved lines and sites the length and breadth of the country. Such has been the enthusiasm for steam that the final chapter - but only of the story so far - looks at examples of the new builds that are taking to the rails - something that epitomises that most valuable human resource - ENTHUSIASM!

2008 BRIDGNORTH

Left: Looking for all the world as though we could be gazing down on a South Wales engine shed, 1928-vintage No 5542 takes a lunchtime break in Bridgnorth shed yard on 19 September 2008 during a visit from the Gloucestershire Warwickshire Steam Railway. All is peace and quiet as it gently releases excess steam, in a glorious external coat, before resuming duties on the main line. Having been despatched to Barry Docks and anticipated scrapping in 1962, it was rescued ten years later, going to the West Somerset Railway. *MJS*

THE FALL OF STEAM 1955-1968

LOUGHBOROUGH

BACKGROUND TO CHANGE 1939-1955

During those dark days between 3 September 1939 and 8 May 1945, when Britain and the railways had been at war, the priority was very much to keep the trains moving at all costs. However, at all costs did not mean literally what perhaps it appeared to - no limit on the money available to spend. 'At all costs' in this period was more to do with clearing the debris of an air raid, and reconnecting the tracks as quickly as possible in order to keep the trains rolling.

With the demands of the war effort requiring much of industry and the available workforce to concentrate on the manufacture of aircraft, ships, armaments, tanks, military vehicles and equipment, the availability of high-quality materials to the railways was severely limited and in reality a regime of 'make do and mend' prevailed.

The railways had been taken under Government control during the war years in order to provide a cohesive system that, while endeavouring to provide as near a normal service as was possible to passengers, was also of course giving due regard and priority to supporting the war effort. The movement of troops and equipment was given priority but, with air raids causing considerable damage, delays were inevitable and travel difficult.

Following the war the assumption that a return to the pre-war privatised 'Big Four' structure of the London Midland & Scottish Railway (LMSR), the Great Western Railway (GWR), the London & North Eastern Railway (LNER) and the Southern Railway (SR) was to prove ill-founded. While the condition of the railway infrastructure going into the war had been far from perfect and varied widely across the country, it is clear that following a period of more intensive usage than ever before seen, coupled with the enforced low maintenance and very little development, the situation on that celebratory VE Day of 8 May 1945 was, for the nation's railways, not so much a celebration of what had passed, but more a fear of what was to come!

Although the railways briefly returned to private ownership, it became apparent that the Government would be unable to afford the huge costs of compensating the owning companies by investing sufficiently to return the infrastructure

In a time warp! It could almost be a platform-end scene on a Southern Region station at any BR period between 1948 and 1968 but is, in fact, looking south at Loughborough Central station deep in the preservation era, in 2009! The locomotive is ex-SR 'King Arthur' 4-6-0 No 30777 *Sir Lamiel*, one of a class of 54 that was the mainstay of routine Southern Railway passenger turns until the advent of Bulleid's 'Pacifics', with steam aplenty as it waits to begin its next run to Leicester North. Built in Scotland at the North British works in June 1925, its final days were spent at Basingstoke shed, from where it was dispensed with in November 1961. Happily, preservation beckoned. *Peter Rowlands*

to its pre-war condition.

The cost of 'buying up' all the shares in the privatised railway companies, based on the pre-war asset value, was by far the cheaper option and could be achieved by the allocation of Government shares in the new British Transport Commission (BTC). The shareholders in the former railway companies were guaranteed a return of 3% per annum on their BTC investment. This was to prove an onerous commitment for the new governing body, but was seen as too little compensation for the railway companies' asset base as assessed on a pre-war valuation.

Thus on 1 January 1948 the Transport Act 1947 became law - the 'Big Four' were no more - the railways were nationalised. Passengers expecting immediate change were to be disappointed; although the 'Big Four' had ceased to exist, they had in fact been replaced by a very similar structure. The trading name chosen for the Railway Executive element of the BTC was simple and to the point - BRITISH RAILWAYS. British Railways was split into six regions: the London Midland Region (LMR), Eastern Region (ER), Western Region (WR), North Eastern Region (NER), Southern Region (SR) and Scottish Region (ScR). These regions were not only similar in area coverage to the old order but also the rolling stock and designs generally stayed in their previous habitats. Although the name BRITISH RAILWAYS would gradually be seen appearing on locomotive tenders and tanks, change was slow to develop, and the first of the memorable 'lion and wheel' designs did not appear widely until 1950 onwards.

Below: Ledbury Town Halt was, as can be seen, a small affair, with a very rudimentary waiting shelter. Situated less than a mile south of the main station in the town, on the single-track GWR branch to Gloucester, the view here is on 4 July 1959, as the guard waits to resume the journey in the ex-GWR Railcar. Passenger services over the route ceased just nine days later, with the stretch to Dymock, some 4 miles south, closing completely. The rest of the branch finally disappeared from the railway system on 30 November 1964. Despite the imminent closure and the quiet nature of the branch, the guard looks creditably smart in his uniform. *MJS collection*

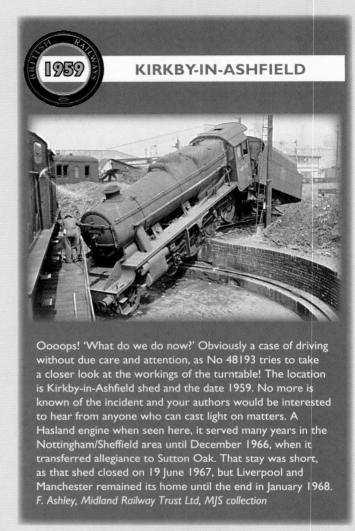

1959 KIRKBY-IN-ASHFIELD

Oooops! 'What do we do now?' Obviously a case of driving without due care and attention, as No 48193 tries to take a closer look at the workings of the turntable! The location is Kirkby-in-Ashfield shed and the date 1959. No more is known of the incident and your authors would be interested to hear from anyone who can cast light on matters. A Hasland engine when seen here, it served many years in the Nottingham/Sheffield area until December 1966, when it transferred allegiance to Sutton Oak. That stay was short, as that shed closed on 19 June 1967, but Liverpool and Manchester remained its home until the end in January 1968. *F. Ashley, Midland Railway Trust Ltd, MJS collection*

1959 LEDBURY TOWN HALT

THE 1955 MODERNISATION PLAN

Behind the scenes, however, Government policy was beginning to formulate and in 1955 the *Modernisation Plan* was published. It was at best a brave attempt to achieve what its title suggested and at worst a major lost opportunity.

The key elements of the plan were contained in a Government white paper published in 1956:

- To return the railways to profit by 1962 - overhauling the deficit announced in 1955/6
- To upgrade lines in the Eastern Region, Kent, Scotland, and the Birmingham area by electrifying the main lines
- To commence a replacement strategy that would over time eliminate steam motive power and replace it with diesel and electric traction
- To provide new passenger and freight rolling stock
- To undertake extensive re-signalling and upgrading/ renewal of track

Below: The notice says it all. D5801 stands at the Brush works in Loughborough on 3 June 1961, during one of the company's Open Days, proudly displayed as 'one of the 226 being supplied to British Railways', with the added note of a 90mph capability. Released to traffic two weeks later, its first allocation was to Stratford, in London, as part of the replacement of steam traction along the ECML and into East Anglia. A move north to Lincoln came two years later and it stayed there for many years. Becoming No 31271 in February 1974, under BR's TOPS system, it remains in operational condition and is normally to be seen at the Midland Railway Centre, Butterley. It was named *Stratford 1841-2001* at York on 31 May 2004. *MJS*

- To close on a selective basis lines that duplicated others and/or those that were deemed as not needed in a national network

The loss of both passenger and freight traffic to road transport was gathering pace and the plan recognised that to win back this vital business the modern railway needed to be more flexible and reliable, and faster. Safety was of course paramount, and the upgrading of track and signalling in particular set out to take account of this. The Government of the day allocated over £1 billion to fund the Modernisation Plan, and it seemed that in principle it was a good one - to make the railway option attractive and preferable based on both speed and efficiency. Why take the car or send goods by road if the rail option was so much quicker and more reliable?

A start was made with the building of new bulk freight handling and sorting facilities, following the decision to remove British Railways' 'common carrier' status, which meant that it had a legal requirement to provide both freight and parcels facilities at virtually all of its stations - large, medium or small. Clearly no such requirement was imposed on the road hauliers.

LOUGHBOROUGH

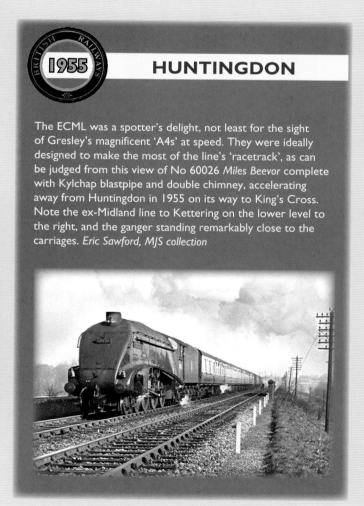

1955   HUNTINGDON

The ECML was a spotter's delight, not least for the sight of Gresley's magnificent 'A4s' at speed. They were ideally designed to make the most of the line's 'racetrack', as can be judged from this view of No 60026 *Miles Beevor* complete with Kylchap blastpipe and double chimney, accelerating away from Huntingdon in 1955 on its way to King's Cross. Note the ex-Midland line to Kettering on the lower level to the right, and the ganger standing remarkably close to the carriages. *Eric Sawford, MJS collection*

Two major factors can serve to keep a railway open – large numbers of fare-paying customers (passengers or freight) or serving a social need. The scenery here certainly does not fulfil the first category, but the wilds of the Highlands certainly need the railway, not least in winter. The Drumochter Pass, between Perth and Aviemore, is extremely isolated but is the primary pass from south to north in the Central Highlands, and has been since prehistoric times. The main A9 road accompanies the railway and both have their summits here – 1,508 and 1,484 feet respectively – with the railway being the highest in the UK. On an unidentified date in 1953, 'Black Five' No 44722 slogs up the gradient with a none-too-long but quite mixed freight. *Doug Giles, MJS collection*

Thus many stations began to lose their goods offices and yards. This in turn meant large reductions in staff and the removal of many slow-moving and often constantly stopping goods trains. The 'pick-up goods', so named because it would proceed from station to station along a route and collect however many wagons each station had ready for despatch, was to become a thing of the past.

The theory was that by reducing the number of stations at which freight was handled, and by building larger main yards with modern equipment - marshalling yards - the much-needed speeding up and greater efficiencies would be achieved.

Hindsight is, of course, a marvellous thing, and there are many reasons why rail traffic continued to decline while road haulage continued to increase. However, your authors, while resisting the temptation to proffer another theory, will try to restrict themselves to a few observations:

- Should money have been spent on speeding up freight handling at small and medium-sized stations rather than on large yards?
- Given that fewer stations were contributing wagons to the main yards, were new main yards needed?
- Would money have been better spent modernising stations and increasing service frequency and relevance?
- Should the rush to remove steam from the network have been slowed to allow more intensive evaluation of the alternatives?
- Should the Government have decreed that closed line trackbeds should have been preserved and not built on, in case of future need?

Throughout the 1950s the slow but sure pattern of railway closures began to increase in frequency as the Modernisation Plan began to take effect. The closing of smaller stations and goods yards, it could be argued, helped drive more passengers and freight to the road hauliers.

The Reshaping of British Railways - The 1963 Report

The next major Government review soon followed. *The Reshaping of British Railways* was published in 1963.

Dr Richard Beeching had been appointed Chairman of British Railways in March 1961 in succession to Sir Brian Robertson. *The Reshaping of British Railways*, prepared at Dr Beeching's behest, was intended to be the new cornerstone on which the future of the railways was to be built. Rather than a further report prepared for the railway by railwaymen, this was to be a far more clinical and business-based approach. Dr Beeching was after all an accomplished business leader and scientist, having been drafted in by the Government from ICI. His approach was far more based on the economics and efficiency of running a railway. This led to controversial surveys throughout the railway, region by region and line by line - men and women with clipboards logging passenger numbers and station usage. Controversial, because of questions relating to the timing of a particular survey, and the ensuing translation of the results. Conspiracy theories were numerous, ranging from the plausible to the utterly far-fetched. In essence, the report argued that providing a service was all well and good but it had to pay its way.

Following publication of the new report the rate of closures was to escalate dramatically

Nothing lasts forever! 'West Country' Class 4-6-2 No 34032 *Camelford* is seen at Southampton's famous Ocean Terminal shortly after arrival with the Queen Elizabeth Boat Express. The Ocean Terminal is no more, having been demolished in 1983, and RMS *Queen Elizabeth* no longer calls; she made her last voyage across the Atlantic in November 1968, meeting her end on 9 January 1971 in Hong Kong harbour, when fire destroyed her. No 34032 was withdrawn from Salisbury shed in November 1966 and went to the breakers shortly after. *Ray Ruffell, Silver Link collection*

1965 SOUTHAMPTON Docks

dramatically and would continue throughout the 1960s. Dr Beeching's report recommended the closure of some 6,000 route miles of Britain's then total route mileage of close to 18,000. The closures would prune from the network mainly rural branches, lines that were considered to be duplicating services, and cross-country lines. In addition, more than 2,000 stations on lines that were to be kept open were also to be closed, thereby speeding up the core services between larger towns and cities.

A second report published just a year later in 1964 was even more savage in its proposals.

The Development of the Major Railway Trunk Route

This, if it had been implemented in full, would have resulted in all lines apart from the major intercity routes and important profit-making commuter lines around the big cities being closed! Britain would today have but a skeleton railway system with even larger areas of the country left entirely without access to the rail network. This further report was rejected by the Government, and Dr Beeching resigned in 1965. It is easy to see why the report has commonly been referred to as the 'Beeching Axe' over the ensuing years.

Following Beeching's departure, the closure programme that he started under a Conservative Government in the early 1960s continued under the Labour administration, only finally slowing to a virtual halt by the mid-1970s. Thus by 1975 the network had been pruned to its current circa 12,000 route miles. Back in 1955, when the first Modernisation Plan was published, the route mileage was closer to 20,000 and the nation had the use of around 4,000 more stations.

As we will see in the following chapters, subsequent to the report's publication steam was rapidly to be eliminated on the national network (with the exception of the Vale of Rheidol narrow gauge line) within 5 years. A number of closed lines have been preserved and reopened as heritage

railways - thriving in part, ironically, on one key element that was proffered as being in vital need of replacement in the interest of modernisation - the steam locomotive.

With the benefit of hindsight, no end of communities the length and breadth of the country will testify that the closure of their local branch line or cross-country railway has proved to have been misjudged. When the lines closed there were considerable protests and public enquiries, for the most part to no avail. Those protesters, many of whom are alive today and still actively seeking reinstatement, tried in vain to convince the powers that be that road traffic congestion would eventually gain a stranglehold. They ventured to suggest that moving freight by rail used one, perhaps two, diesel engines, whereas the same load hauled by road can require the use of many, many more diesel engines. All this before global warming and ecological effects really entered the public consciousness!

The freight carried by rail today is confined to longer-distance bulk loads. Long gone are the days when you could turn up at your local station with virtually anything from a feather to an elephant and expect the railway to accept it and send it off to anywhere in the country! Interestingly, in a way the steam-age pick-up goods still operates, but now by road.

Parcel companies pick up goods from business premises in vans and take them to a local depot where they are off-loaded and reloaded on to articulated trunkers that carry combined loads either to a large regional hub for further trans-shipment between trunkers or direct to local depots where they are off-loaded and reloaded on to the delivery vans that then deliver them to business premises. Does this not seem all too familiar? Indeed, we are gradually seeing a return of freight to the railways with large road hauliers now using dedicated trains on selected long-distance routes.

The many years of change since the demise of steam have seen greater automation and computerised handling, which ensures a smoother and swifter operation - we can only speculate as to how many lines could have been saved had these developments come sooner and been fully applied at the local level.

1963   HAYLING ISLAND

Class A1X 'Terrier' No 32670 is in charge of the last passenger train to Hayling Island – 'The Hayling Farewell' – is seen at the terminus on 3 November 1963. The line was just 4½ miles in length, featuring an 1,100-foot wooden trestle viaduct - including an opening section made of steel - to provide access to Langstone harbour. The cost of maintaining the viaduct was a key factor in the decision to close the line. The goods shed still stands today as part of the Station Theatre and is run by Hayling Island Amateur Dramatic Society. *Ray Ruffell/Silver Link Archive*

The SOUTHERN Region 1955 – 1967

Compared to the three other major regions – GWR, LMSR and LNER – the Southern and Scottish areas were minnows. Whilst the geographical span was not inconsiderable in both cases, the number of locomotives operated was small by comparison and, in the latter's case, many were imported designs from south of the border. The Southern did have its own indigenous stock, which remained confined within borders with just a handful of workings that saw its engines sneak into adjacent regions; but what it did have in abundance, due to its proximity to London south of the Thames and the near-claustrophobic conurbations

Above: The 'hoody' and the photographer in the foreground, who is standing on the edge of a large puddle, indicate that the weather conditions for this LCGB rail tour were not the most pleasurable, or conducive to good photography! On 22 January 1967 'Mickey Mouse' No 41295 stands at the terminus at Bridport, giving participants the opportunity of visiting this threatened station. The 'Bridport Belle' tour had begun at Waterloo and employed six steam locomotives and one diesel during the itinerary. Arrival at Bridport was an hour late, due to the discovery of a dead body on the train – see http://www.sixbellsjunction.co.uk and the link to 'railtours' for a fuller story! Freight had already been withdrawn from the branch and it finally closed on 5 May 1975. *MJS collection*

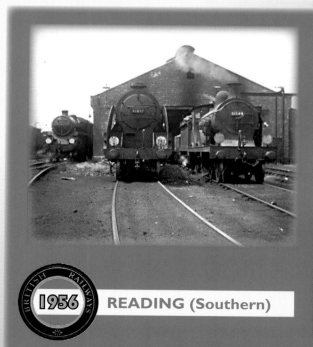

Left: It is June 1956 and the Southern shed in Reading houses (l-r) Nos 76058, 30837 and 31549, while *(below)* on another occasion in the same year three different types are present, Nos 30718, 31898 and 33002. Opened by the SER in 1875 to replace earlier facilities, and with a 65-foot turntable, these views show the then new gable ends. Closure came in 1965. *Both Ray Ruffell, Silver Link collection*

within Kent, Surrey, Sussex and Hampshire, was hundreds of thousands of commuters travelling to 'the smoke' every day. Its network, therefore, was the most cramped anywhere in the UK and the demands this put on men and machines cannot be overestimated; but it also had fingers further west, not least to the seaside resorts along the South Coast to Devon.

Formed in 1923, it inherited many ancient locomotives from the SE&CR, LB&SCR and LSWR and many of these survived to serve the new master after Nationalisation in 1948, but as early as the 1930s it was seen that new types were needed, despite the introduction and on-going spread of electrification that encompassed the vast majority of the suburban commuting network by that time. Its own workshops turned out successful and radical designs over the two decades to Nationalisation, then continued to supply the new British Railways for a further period.

BR(S) inherited around 1,850 locomotives in 1948 and the decline in this number was slow in the first years of British Railways, partly helped by new locos coming on stream from pre-Nationalisation orders and the introduction of some of the new 'Standard' engines now being built. By 1955 this figure was in the region of 1,300, a 30% decline largely dictated by the disappearance of the older types and the

Below: For many years both before and after Nationalisation in 1948, a number of railway works employed ancient locos, put out to grass from front-line services, to shunt the 'dead' engines around the sites. One of those employed at Brighton was ex-Stroudley 'A1X' 'Terrier' No 377S, at some time numbered DS377, seen on site on 5 May 1957. Of a type introduced in 1911, as a rebuild with an extended smokebox, it served Brighton Works until 11 March 1959, when it was somewhat surprisingly restored to normal traffic – as No 32635 – and transferred to Brighton shed. The end was to come on 29 April 1963. *Gerald Adams, MJS collection*

BRIGHTON

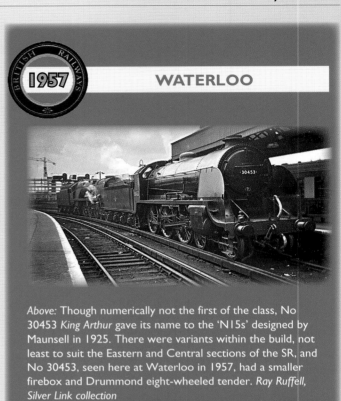

WATERLOO

Above: Though numerically not the first of the class, No 30453 *King Arthur* gave its name to the 'N15s' designed by Maunsell in 1925. There were variants within the build, not least to suit the Eastern and Central sections of the SR, and No 30453, seen here at Waterloo in 1957, had a smaller firebox and Drummond eight-wheeled tender. *Ray Ruffell, Silver Link collection*

HAYLING ISLAND

Above: No 32640 had a very chequered career! One of Stroudley's 'Terriers' for the LB&SCR, it was originally No 40 and named *Brighton*, then IWCR 11 named *Newport*, then SR 2640 and finally with its BR number, as seen here at Hayling Island on 10 June 1957. Built at Brighton Works in 1878, it moved to the Isle of Wight in 1902, and was reboilered as an 'A1X' with an enlarged bunker and equipped for 'push-pull' duties in 1918. A return to the mainland came in 1947 and a career on the Hayling Island shuttle service. Withdrawn on 14 October 1963, it was saved by Billy Butlin and subsequently transferred to the Isle of Wight Steam Railway in 1976. *Ray Ruffell, Silver Link collection*

1956 READING (Southern)

BRITISH RAILWAYS

Left: Another view of Reading's Southern shed, again in June 1956, highlights No 31549 of the trio seen on the bottom left on page 11. One of a 4-4-0 design from Wainwright for the SE&CR in 1901, it retained its rather antiquated curves throughout, unlike some that were rebuilt by Maunsell from 1921 onwards. Ending up at Guildford in September 1955 — its shed here - it was withdrawn three months after this view and scrapped. *Ray Ruffell, Silver Link collection*

1964 SALISBURY

Below: Fresh out of the workshops, 'King Arthur' No 30793 *Sir Ontzlake* truly looks in magnificent condition and raring to go! Standing in line at Eastleigh Works on 9 July 1957 with others fresh from attention, it awaits a fire to be lit, a run back to Stewarts Lane shed and front-line working. Built in 1926, it was one of the last of the class to go, being withdrawn from Basingstoke on 24 September 1962, after a sojourn of 18 months and a similar stay previously at Feltham. *MJS collection*

Right: Sunday 20 September 1964 saw the Southern Counties Touring Society run a 'Farewell to Steam' tour from Victoria to Seaton and back, departing at 9.33am and due back at 7.43pm. However, final arrival back in London was actually at 8.22pm, due to a diversion from the planned route between Staines Central and Clapham Junction. The lion's share of the haulage was handled by No. 92220 *Evening Star*, which is seen leaving Salisbury, adorned with an appropriate headboard. *Ray Ruffell, Silver Link collection*

1957 EASTLEIGH

GUILDFORD

Guildford was one of a small handful of 'half roundhouse' engine sheds, nestling under the chalk cliff to the south of the station. On Good Friday, 16 April 1965, No 34005 *Barnstaple* stands by the shedmaster's office before leaving for the next duty. It served a variety of (mainly LSWR) sheds before suffering withdrawal at Bournemouth on 14 November 1966, eight months from the end of steam on the SR. *Ray Ruffell, Silver Link collection*

1966 VAUXHALL

Without doubt, the stirring sight of a steam locomotive working hard can bring shivers to the spine, even to those who were born too late to know it for real. On 1 June 1966 the fireman of No 73155 is obviously hard at it as his train accelerates away from Waterloo and into Vauxhall, on its journey south as the 12.35pm to Weymouth.

Note the scorching of the smokebox door and the absence of a shedplate, which should have been showing allegiance to Eastleigh shed. New in January 1957, it survived just ten years to the end of steam on the SR, before withdrawal from Guildford on 9 July 1967, adding to the collection of BR's wasted assets.
Dennis Weaver, MJS collection

continual spread of electrification, as well as closure of some less economic lines and/or operations; several classes had become extinct.

The effects of the 1955 Modernisation Plan were slow to make inroads, as elsewhere in the country, but this began to change as the decade drew to a close, so that by the end of 1960 there were just 45 classes left, many with just one or two members battling on, and the sum total was now down to around 900 (yet another 30% reduction). This year was to be pivotal; as *Evening Star* emerged from Swindon Works as the last steam loco built for BR, the writing was well and truly on the wall for steam, although the speed of the end was still as yet not anticipated.

Perhaps surprisingly, despite the relatively few numbers of engines extant, the tentacles of electrification spreading further and other regions seeing the end of steam altogether, the Southern was to be one of the last to be finally cleansed. True, the number of locos halved in just two years to the

Below: 'The South Western Suburban Railtour' of 5 February 1967 was the LCGB's 100th rail tour, leaving Waterloo at 8.45am behind No 77014 and visiting a myriad of south London sites, including Windsor and even reaching Reading. 'Standard 4' 2-6-4T No 80145 came on to the train at Wimbledon Park at 10.04am and this view is thought to be at that changeover point, with a healthy crowd to witness the event. This loco took the train to Shepperton. Leaving this changeover just 2 minutes down, Waterloo was regained 10 late, at 6.15pm, but considering the convoluted itinerary and the number of loco changes this was a very creditable effort by all concerned. *MJS collection*

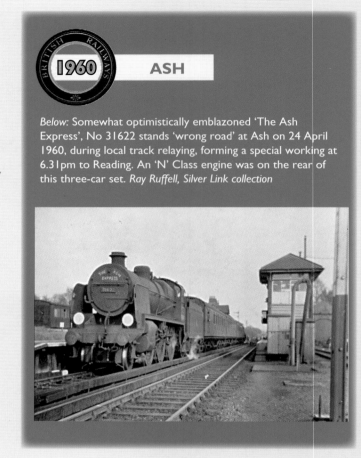

1960 ASH

Below: Somewhat optimistically emblazoned 'The Ash Express', No 31622 stands 'wrong road' at Ash on 24 April 1960, during local track relaying, forming a special working at 6.31pm to Reading. An 'N' Class engine was on the rear of this three-car set. *Ray Ruffell, Silver Link collection*

1967 WIMBLEDON PARK

1964 EASTLEIGH

Right: One of your authors was the founder of the Thurmaston Railway Society, to enable him and others to visit locations/sheds of choice and including many that other clubs/societies in and around Leicester seemed not to visit! Travelling by coach, the trip of 21 June 1964 encompassed sheds in the Southern Region and was blessed with good weather. Seen at Eastleigh, 'Battle of Britain' No 34076 *41 Squadron,* complete with squadron crest, stands by the starter signal awaiting the call to duty. Still in its original 'air-smoothed' form, it was withdrawn from Salisbury on 10 January 1966, just 17½ years after it began life in June 1948. *MJS*

Below: Slightly earlier in the day, the TRS had reached the southernmost location on this day and had toured Bournemouth shed. Members of the club can be seen busy scribbling down the engine numbers as they wander round. No 82027 was new

in December 1954 and allocated to the North East, where it stayed until a dramatic move south, together with sisters Nos 82026/28/29, in September 1963. It here stands proudly in the yard, midway through a brief eight-month stint at Bournemouth. *MJS*

1964 BOURNEMOUTH

end of 1962, with the number of classes equally scythed, but it was to be the summer of 1967 before the Grim Reaper was finally successful. Branch-line closures further hastened the end, atop the introduction of the successful BRCW Type 3s (later Class 33s) from 1960 – 98 were in service within two years! – so that by the turn of 1967 just six classes were still in service, totalling 66 examples. There was one glimmer of hope, however. The fledgling Bluebell Railway Preservation Society had plans in 1960 to reopen the branch line south from East Grinstead through Sheffield Park, which became its headquarters. It perforce had to change plans over time, but has not been defeated in much of

EASTLEIGH

1964

Two more views from the Thurmaston Railway Society trip of 21 June 1964, again at Eastleigh.

Left: Once named *Granville* (removed in January 1951), ex-LSWR 'B4' 0-4-0T No 30102 stands, withdrawn, on the scrap line, awaiting its fate. Designed for dock shunting, the class was introduced by Adams in 1891 and 102 was one of the last to be built, in December 1893. Having spent many years working out of Plymouth (Friary) shed, it transferred to Eastleigh in October 1958 and stayed there until withdrawal on 14 October 1963, apart from 2½ years at Bournemouth from March 1959. Sold by BR following withdrawal, it was placed on display at Butlin s Camp in Ayr from October 1964. *MJS*

Left: 'Terrier' No 32662 stands just in front of No 30102 and was to share the same fate! Serving Fratton at Nationalisation, 1953 saw it travel to pastures new – St Leonard's – in October, and Brighton two months later, before joining the 'B4' at Eastleigh on 27 May 1963. Its deletion from stock came on 9 December of that year, with the trip to Scotland to follow. *MJS*

Below: The fact that it is towards the latter days of steam on BR is betrayed by the absence of nameplates on 'Britannia' No 70002 *Geoffrey Chaucer*, as it stands in Waterloo – with a 12A Carlisle (Kingmoor) shedplate proudly displayed on the smokebox! – on 12 May 1966, waiting to take the 9.20am 'United States Boat Express' to Southampton. This is quite rightly – as denoted by the headcode disc – a special working! *Ray Ruffell, Silver Link collection*

what it proposed, and still has on-going aspirations. *See the story later in this volume.*

So, following hot on the heels of the official end of steam on the Scottish Region the previous month, the axe finally fell on Southern metals on 9 July 1967, when enthusiasts flocked from around the country to witness the sad demise and the last BR steam running into and out of Waterloo.

LONDON (Waterloo)

1966

The WESTERN Region 1955 - 1965

The Western Region was unique among the 'Big Four' at Nationalisation in 1948, in the form of its heritage. It could trace its birth back to the 1830s, and was the sole member of the 'Big Four' that existed as an entity prior to 1923; its major locomotives could trace their history over a long lineage, right back to Daniel Gooch; it avoided any BR

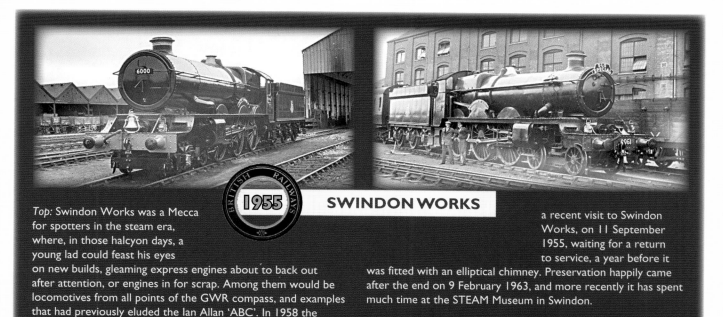

1955 SWINDON WORKS

Top: Swindon Works was a Mecca for spotters in the steam era, where, in those halcyon days, a young lad could feast his eyes on new builds, gleaming express engines about to back out after attention, or engines in for scrap. Among them would be locomotives from all points of the GWR compass, and examples that had previously eluded the Ian Allan 'ABC'. In 1958 the 'gleaming beasts' are represented by No 5094 *Tretower Castle*; looking in glorious condition and obviously near the end of its visit, it will soon be returning to Gloucester (Horton Road) shed. New in June 1939, it was still a relatively young engine when it was withdrawn in September 1962. *Rodney Deval, MJS collection*

Above left: Probably the most celebrated GWR loco is No 6000 *King George V*. New in June 1927 and named after the reigning monarch, it was sent as an exhibit to the Baltimore & Ohio Railroad centenary exhibition of September 1927, where it was endowed with the obligatory US bell. Here it stands after a recent visit to Swindon Works, on 11 September 1955, waiting for a return to service, a year before it was fitted with an elliptical chimney. Preservation happily came after the end on 9 February 1963, and more recently it has spent much time at the STEAM Museum in Swindon.

Above right: The 'Stars' were the forerunners of the very successful 'Castles', but although very capable engines their age told against them and only a handful survived into British Railways days. No 4061 *Glastonbury Abbey* was new from Swindon in May 1922 and lasted until February 1957, working out its days at Wolverhampton (Stafford Road) shed. On the same day as the view of No 6000, it rests outside the Works at Swindon before resuming its rail tour duty. This SLS (Midland Area) 'Star Special' ran from Birmingham (Snow Hill) to Swindon and back – out via Stratford-upon-Avon and Cheltenham and back via Didcot and Oxford. *Both Gerald Adams, MJS collection*

A wonderful evocation of what we have lost since the demise of the steam engine on Britain's railways. As well as the living, breathing creature that is here taking water, we have the semaphore signal, a large running-in board announcing connections that could be made at Builth Road High Level station, and the general station architecture that is sadly missing so often today. The fireman chats to the Station Master in the summer of 1958 as No 48895 has its tender water tank replenished. Being an ex-LNWR design, it retains that company's tradition of not providing a front number; it is also without a formal shedplate, with merely a stencil denoting its 8F Wigan (Spring's Branch) allocation. Built in May 1904 and receiving its BR number in November 1948, it was the last of its class, withdrawn on Boxing Day 1964, the same day as three classmates. The class is represented in preservation by No 49395 in the National Collection. *MJS collection*

renumbering; and it kept the GWR numberplate style, ie a plate affixed to the cabside rather than the number painted on. This saved the new administration a great amount of work and money; enabled the enthusiasts to know immediately whether they had seen a particular locomotive before without checking their 'ABCs'; and allowed GWR aficionados to have an even more elevated opinion of these survivors of 'God's Wonderful Railway'.

Of the 20,076 steam engines inherited by BR, the Western Region laid claim to 3,856 - 19.2% - more than double the number encompassed within the Southern section. By the end of 1955 this number had only fallen to 3,458 – a mere 10% over eight complete years – and only a relative handful of classes had become extinct. As with the Southern, the vast majority of casualties were the more ancient pre-First World War types and many from the smaller railways that had

been absorbed at the 1923 Grouping. It was to be the early 1960s before the axe began to swing much more rapidly.

Swindon Works was the hub of its character and existence, with its creations still undertaking the most demanding of duties and being the envy of many; its design basics and flair had even been 'exported' to the LMS through Stanier. Under BR(W), the GWR map was virtually unchanged in the first years, and to all intents and purposes it was 'GWR' in all but name, with named expresses, South Wales valleys' workings and holiday trains packed solid with travellers

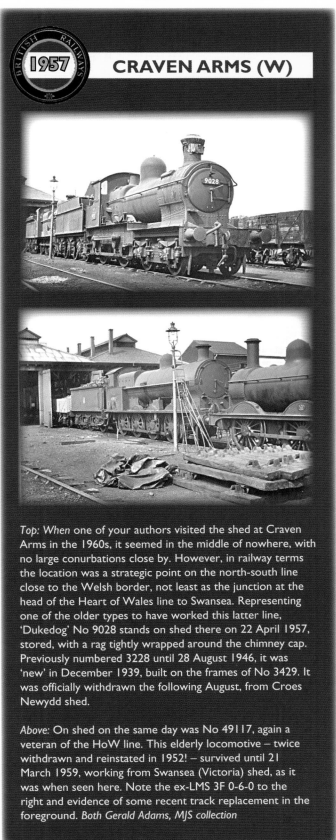

1957 CRAVEN ARMS (W)

1958 BUILTH ROAD (High Level)

Top: When one of your authors visited the shed at Craven Arms in the 1960s, it seemed in the middle of nowhere, with no large conurbations close by. However, in railway terms the location was a strategic point on the north-south line close to the Welsh border, not least as the junction at the head of the Heart of Wales line to Swansea. Representing one of the older types to have worked this latter line, 'Dukedog' No 9028 stands on shed there on 22 April 1957, stored, with a rag tightly wrapped around the chimney cap. Previously numbered 3228 until 28 August 1946, it was 'new' in December 1939, built on the frames of No 3429. It was officially withdrawn the following August, from Croes Newydd shed.

Above: On shed on the same day was No 49117, again a veteran of the HoW line. This elderly locomotive – twice withdrawn and reinstated in 1952! – survived until 21 March 1959, working from Swansea (Victoria) shed, as it was when seen here. Note the ex-LMS 3F 0-6-0 to the right and evidence of some recent track replacement in the foreground. *Both Gerald Adams, MJS collection*

into Devon and Cornwall all operating as they had prior to 1948. Some GWR classes were still being built up to 1956 without a break! The Works was also involved in new builds and all seemed to be progressing satisfactorily enough, but the warning of great change came with the emergence from Swindon of the very last steam engine built for BR – No 92220 *Evening Star,* named on 18 March 1960 – and, ironically, the 999th and last 'Standard' constructed.

As a new decade loomed, straws in the wind of the after-effects of rail strikes, road competition and the

Below: No 92220 *Evening Star* will forever be a celebrity, as the last steam locomotive built by British Railways, completed at Swindon Works and named there on 18 March 1960. As befitted its unique status, it was painted in lined green livery and adorned with a pseudo-GWR copper-capped chimney, the only one of the class to be so privileged. Consequently, although it served the railway in the same way as the rest of the 249 'Standard' 9Fs, it was always a delight to spotters. Though close to the end of its all-too-short BR career – just five years! – it was still in fine external condition when seen at Cardiff East Dock shed on 12 July 1964. *MJS*

Above: Another SLS Special, with yet another ancient type at the helm. On 21 May 1955 No 2516 pauses at Kidderminster at around 4pm with the Society's 'West Midland Rail Tour' from Birmingham (Snow Hill) to Ditton Priors and back. Note that, in an attempt at recreating past practice, the number has been added to the bufferbeam and the smokebox number and shedplate have both been blacked out! Built at Swindon Works in March 1897, the end came just under a year from this portrait, following which it was preserved and now resides in the STEAM Museum in Swindon. *Gerald Adams, MJS collection*

1955 **KIDDERMINSTER**

1964 **CARDIFF EAST DOCK**

A major stop in Wales for the 'Cambrian Coast Express' was at Welshpool. Initially on the Cambrian Railways route between Oswestry and the coast, its junction status was from the spur branching off to Shrewsbury, as confirmed by the names announced on the running-in board on the left. Double-headed on a Shrewsbury-Aberystwyth turn five years on from the view above, on 15 August 1964, Nos 7820 *Dinmore Manor*, taking water, and 7806 *Cockington Manor* pause before resuming their trek west. While a station still serves the town, it is now to the right of this view, with the erstwhile trackbed converted to form a road by-pass. *MJS collection*

Above: One of the delights of steam days was the presence throughout the country of named expresses, with large headboards adorning the smokebox front. One that received much affectionate interest, not just among GWR aficionados, was the 'Cambrian Coast Express'. Introduced mainly for holiday traffic, the first official use of the name was in 1927, when the train ran only on Summer Fridays and Saturdays. Subsequent pre-war and post-war periods saw changes, but the predominant service was via Shrewsbury to Aberystwyth and Pwllheli, utilising through coaches detached as appropriate at Machynlleth. On 14 August 1959 No 5006 *Tregenna Castle* awaits the green light at Paddington station, at the start of the train's journey of more than 5 hours. *MJS collection*

need for economies came with smaller shed facilities closing, such as Watlington (1957), Henley-on-Thames (1958) and Wallingford (1956) in the London area, and Ashburton (1958), Minehead (1956) and Plymouth (Princetown, 1956) 'out west'. But it would be 1961 and 1963 that would see more seismic upheavals. Many of the WR sheds closed and/or were shuffled to new controlling depots, and in the latter year those in the West Midlands transferred allegiance to the LMR and others were re-coded. Reduction of working locos was still initially gradual – a drop of only 2,613 to 2,437 (9.3%) in 1961 – but this had fallen more dramatically to 1,276 (just short of 48%!) two years later.

Just as dramatic was the dispensing with the mighty 'Kings'. Falling foul of the introduction of diesels – the D8XX 'Warships' from August 1958, D70XX 'Hymeks' (May 1961) and D10XX 'Westerns' (December 1961) – the end was spectacular. The first to go – No 6006 *King George I* in February 1962 from Wolverhampton (Stafford Road) shed – was followed by the whole class within just 12 months! 'Castles', 'Halls', 'Granges' and 'Manors' escaped this awful

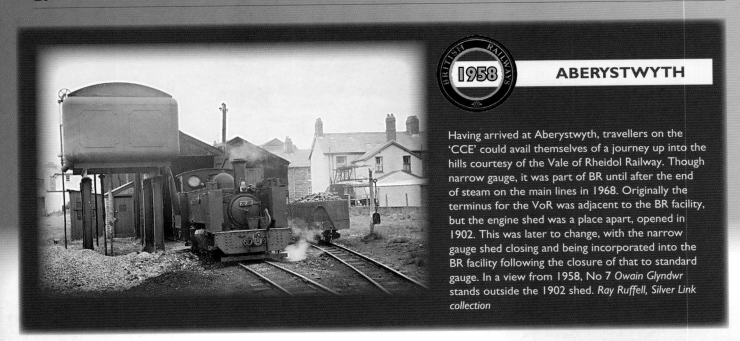

1958 ABERYSTWYTH

Having arrived at Aberystwyth, travellers on the 'CCE' could avail themselves of a journey up into the hills courtesy of the Vale of Rheidol Railway. Though narrow gauge, it was part of BR until after the end of steam on the main lines in 1968. Originally the terminus for the VoR was adjacent to the BR facility, but the engine shed was a place apart, opened in 1902. This was later to change, with the narrow gauge shed closing and being incorporated into the BR facility following the closure of that to standard gauge. In a view from 1958, No 7 *Owain Glyndwr* stands outside the 1902 shed. *Ray Ruffell, Silver Link collection*

1964 DIDCOT

Main picture: Over the past 40 years or so, Didcot has developed into a fitting headquarters for the Great Western Society, having taken over the old BR engine shed and moved into the 21st century with progress to suit the modern appetite but without losing the real flavour of GWR operations. On 11 October 1964 Percy Franklin, one of the members of the Thurmaston Railway Society visiting the shed, makes full use of his light meter before taking his photograph of No 4959 *Purley Hall*. Other members can be seen in the background, about to enter the shed building to capture more numbers. Spending much of its BR life around Wolverhampton, Birmingham and Bristol, No 4959 moved to Didcot in October 1958 and worked out its term there until 23 January 1965. The cutter's torch did its work at J. Buttigieg's Newport scrapyard just two months later. *MJS*

fate, but their numbers declined rapidly from 1961; the last 'Castle' went in 1964, and the others in 1965. Steam was officially eradicated from the WR by 31 December 1965 and the only ex-GWR locos still in operation were at the by now LMR-controlled depots. The condition of many working in those last days, however, was a poor representative of a once mighty empire, being devoid of both front and cabside numberplates and in appalling external condition, but the pride of the men working them was as strong as ever.

1964

SWINDON WORKS

We have seen pristine locomotives at Swindon Works, and now it is the turn of the condemned. Looking decidedly down at heel on 22 March 1964, No 4275 stands in the yard, with other unfortunates, waiting for the acetylene torch. Connecting rods are tied to the bufferbeam; the boiler valve casing is missing; the smokebox is showing signs of wear; and rust is gathering. Having spent virtually the whole of its life in the South Wales valleys, its last home was at Neath, from where it had been withdrawn two months before this shot. Strangely, this was not to be its last port of call, as it was transferred to R. & S. Hayes (later Birds Commercial Motors) at Bridgend, where it was cut in September 1964. *MJS*

BLAENAU FFESTINIOG

The furthest GWR outpost in north-west Wales was at Blaenau Ffestiniog, on a branch from Bala. There was also an ex-LMS presence in the town, but in BR days the two did not meet, although the Ffestiniog Railway did serve both on its route through the town! Freight was a lifeblood of the GWR branch, as can be seen from this view of No 8791 leaving Blaenau with a decidedly mixed rake of vehicles on 4 April 1959. Stationed at Stourbridge Junction in 1948, a move into Wales came with transfer to Croes Newydd on 11 August 1956. Bala was a sub-shed of Croes, hence the appearance here at Blaenau. March 1961 saw No 8791 move south to Cardiff, before later moves brought it to Neath in May 1962 and the end there on 9 March 1963. *Gerald Adams, MJS collection*

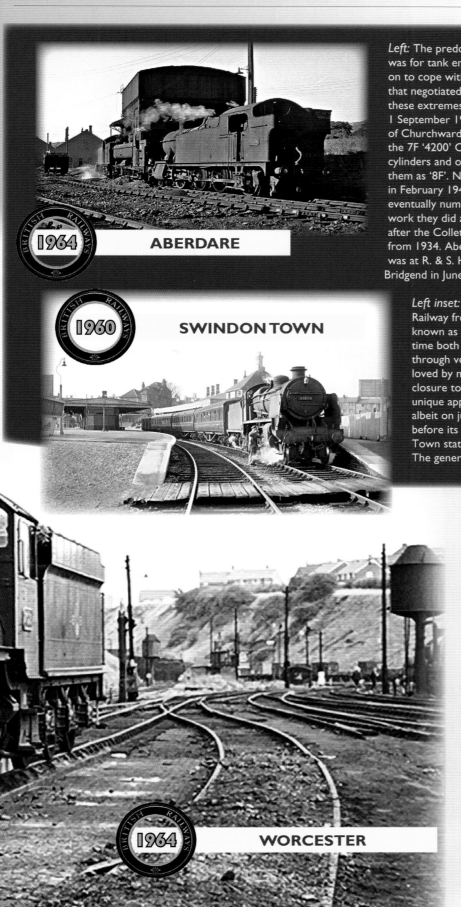

1964 ABERDARE

1960 SWINDON TOWN

1964 WORCESTER

Left: The predominant need in the South Wales valleys was for tank engines of varying sizes that could be relied on to cope with both heavy loads and the twisting track that negotiated the sometimes tortuous terrain. Two of these extremes of design are side by side at Aberdare on 1 September 1964. Closest to the camera is No 5256, one of Churchward's designs. Originally introduced in 1910 as the 7F '4200' Class, 1923 saw a development with enlarged cylinders and other detail alterations, which reclassified them as '8F'. No 5256 was one of the last to be built – new in February 1940, ready for the war effort – of a class eventually numbering 151. They were very successful in the work they did and continued to give first-class service even after the Collett derivation 8F '7200' Class began to appear from 1934. Aberdare was its last home and its bitter end was at R. & S. Hayes (later Birds Commercial Motors) in Bridgend in June 1965.

Left inset: The Midland & South Western Junction Railway from Cheltenham to Andover (affectionately known as the 'Tiddly Dyke') was disadvantaged over time both by its GWR neighbour and the fact that it ran through very sparsely populated areas. It was, however, loved by many and is still fondly remembered, long after closure to passengers on 11 September 1961. It had the unique appeal of bringing SR locos into Cheltenham, albeit on just one train a day at the end. In the year before its disappearance, No 31619 pauses at Swindon Town station on 5 March 1960, en route to Andover. The general relaxed air of the line is here reflected in the driver taking time out to undertake a spot of oiling during the stop! *Gerald Adams, MJS collection*

Left main picture: Worcester shed – coded 85A by BR – sat amidst a cat's cradle of lines just north of Shrub Hill station. During a rail tour visit to the shed on 12 July 1964, No 7025 *Sudeley Castle* stands proudly in the shed yard, looking in fine external condition and complete with appropriate shedplate. New on 30 September 1949, built by BR at Swindon to the GWR design, it was another locomotive that was not an economic investment, being withdrawn exactly three months after this view and cut with indecent haste at G. Cohen's Morriston scrapyard in October. To the left is No 6155, resplendent in its green passenger livery. Handling suburban trains into and out of Paddington for much of its early life, it made the long journey to Severn Tunnel Junction shed in February 1956, thence to Taunton 4¼ years later. The move to Worcester was in November 1962, where it was dispensed with just short of three years later. *MJS*

1961 **BARRY**

Left: Over the years, Barry shed was passed by thousands on their way to Butlin's Holiday Camp or to Dai Woodham's scrapyard, and many no doubt managed a visit to the facility. No 3848 stands as a lone presence at the north end of the shed on 2 September 1964, just one week before closure. Happily the building still stands in the 21st century, but not as open as here. *MJS*

Below: Another location that saw visiting engines from the Southern Region was Oxford. The university city was normally where a change of engines occurred, principally on the York-Bournemouth cross-country rosters, with, on the southbound route, the SR taking over from LNER in the heart of GWR territory! In an undated view, but thought to be 1961, 'Lord Nelson' No 30862 *Lord Collingwood* has received the road and begins to move its train away from the station. Note the Gresley coach immediately behind the tender, and the ex-GWR 0-6-0PT waiting in the middle up road for its clearance to complete its trip working to Hinksey yard. *MJS collection*

1961 **OXFORD**

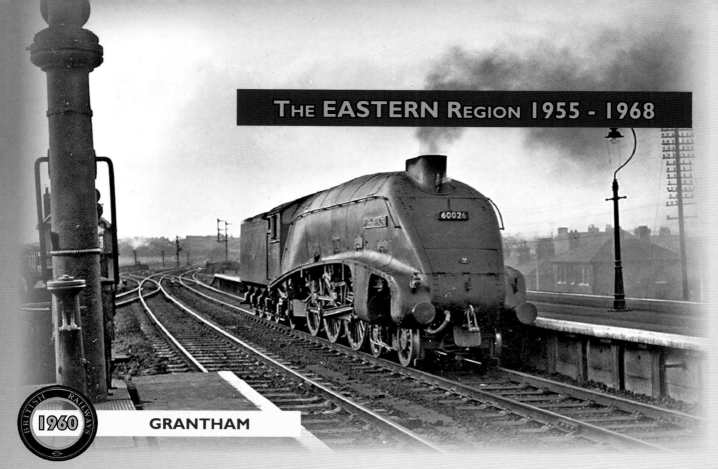

1960 GRANTHAM

At Nationalisation, the ex-LNER grouping included ex-North East and Scottish Divisions and the locomotives within this group were allocated new numbers beginning with a '6'. This was perhaps logical, as the major route out of King's Cross, vying with the LMS 'Premier Line' out of Euston for traffic to north of the border, ran through North Eastern territory to reach Scotland. This group inherited slightly in excess of 6,500 steam locomotives, being just short of 33% of the total handed over to BR and forming the second largest of the 'Big Four'. It was, indeed, a real mix as taken over by BR and, while not exactly a poisoned chalice, it was certainly not an easy grouping to manage. There were areas of heavy industry and sparsely populated rural sections; pockets of commuting and intense roster demands, not least into and out of Liverpool Street; modern express locomotives alongside decidedly ancient, less able stock; and financial problems aplenty, not least through past mismanagement and the after-effects of the Second World War, plus financing the decision to electrify the Sheffield-Manchester 'Woodhead Route'.

No fewer than 153 different classes existed within the group in 1948, excluding variants within classes, again many consisting of a small

As with Oxford on the previous page, Grantham was a staging post, with many trains 'changing horses' here. On 19 August 1960 No 60026 *Miles Beevor* is seen again, drifting from the shed yard into the station before positioning itself at the southern end of the platform to take over an express to King's Cross. The classic, sweeping, streamlined design of Gresley's 'A4s' is vividly demonstrated in this angle. Note the station furniture so common in those times — gas lamp, water column, semaphore signals and the incredibly endowed telegraph pole on the extreme right! *MJS*

1956 CAMBRIDGE

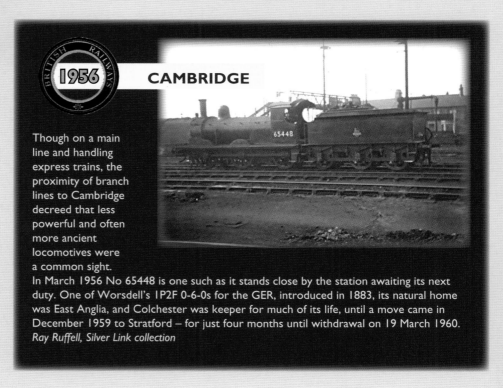

Though on a main line and handling express trains, the proximity of branch lines to Cambridge decreed that less powerful and often more ancient locomotives were a common sight.

In March 1956 No 65448 is one such as it stands close by the station awaiting its next duty. One of Worsdell's 1P2F 0-6-0s for the GER, introduced in 1883, its natural home was East Anglia, and Colchester was keeper for much of its life, until a move came in December 1959 to Stratford — for just four months until withdrawal on 19 March 1960. *Ray Ruffell, Silver Link collection*

handful or even just a single example. Obviously, this was a potential logistical nightmare and one that would need to be dealt with. By the end of 1955 62 locomotives had been consigned to history, including Class 'U1' No 69999, Gresley's massive 2-8-8-2T Garratt built in 1925 for banking the Worsborough Incline east of the Woodhead route. With the electrification of the line in 1953, the loco became redundant. It was tried on the Midland Region's Lickey Incline in 1949 and 1955, converted to oil-burning in the latter year, but without success, and was withdrawn at the end of the year. To slightly counter the reduction in numbers, there was, as with the other regions, a continuation of building older types, with a total by 1952 of 368 'A2s', 'B1s', 'K1s' and 'L1s'; however, by the end of 1955 the total had fallen to just short

of 5,100 – a decline of 22% in just eight years – and the next eight would see a much greater transformation. While not having a major influence initially, 'tweaking' of the region's boundaries came in 1957, when the LMR was the beneficiary of the former GCR route out of Marylebone. Perhaps understandably, the LMR preferred its own locomotive types and thus the ER cause was not helped.

Elsewhere, the introduction of diesel multiple units (DMUs) and a variety of Type 2 diesels on the part-underground services from Moorgate and other commuting turns out of King's Cross to the suburbs dealt a blow to the condensing-apparatus-fitted 'N2s'. The 1956 electrification to Southend

1960   GRANTHAM

Another view of Grantham on 19 August 1960 shows No 60067 *Ladas,* complete with 'German Federal'-type smoke deflectors, fitted in the late 1950s, also slowly drifting along the up platform in readiness to relieve another London-bound train. As an indication that Gresley's 'A3s' were regarded as racehorses of the East Coast Main Line, with their professed and acknowledged speed, the majority of the class were named after famous race winners from the past. *Ladas,* owned by the 5th Earl of Rosebery, was the winner of the 1894 Epsom Derby, ridden by John Watts and trained by Mathew Dawson, who also trained the same stable's 'Sir Visto' the following year. This latter horse was the name given to the next 'A3' in line, No 60068. *MJS*

1961   ESSENDINE

Above: For historical reasons, Retford enjoyed the services of two distinct engine sheds, one ex-GNR and the other ex-GCR. The latter is seen on 14 June 1964, with stored No 63726 in company with classmate 63914 and an ex-WD 'Austerity' 2-8-0. Standing under the sheerlegs – not an uncommon sight at ex-GC sheds – No 63726 is adorned with a 'NOT TO BE MOVED' plate, not surprisingly as it had been withdrawn the previous month. Note the crazy angle of the left-hand buffer and the buckle of the running plate, presumably a sign of hard knocks along the way! No 63914's tender is piled high with coal, but it is doubtful if the loco actually again moved 'in anger', as it had been withdrawn officially the day before this view! Situated to the east of Retford station, on the south side of the Gainsborough line, the shed was officially 'Retford Thrumpton', opening in July 1849 and surviving until closure in January 1965. *MJS*

Left: Another 'A4', this time at top speed. Passing a decidedly derelict house, No 60024 *Kingfisher* roars down the hill at Essendine on 7 August 1961, at the head of the up 'Elizabethan' express. Initiated in the 1950s, to celebrate the 'new Elizabethan era' following the coronation of Queen Elizabeth II, the train ran non-stop between King's Cross and Edinburgh in both directions. Gresley's 'A4s' were entrusted to the roster and they and the train became celebrated through the initiative. 1961 was the last year that it was steam-hauled, with the massive 'Deltics' taking over from the following year. A Scottish-allocated engine for the majority of its life, No 60024 ended its days on 24 September 1966, together with sisters Nos 60019 *Bittern* and 60034 *Lord Faringdon*, at Aberdeen (Ferryhill) shed. *MJS*

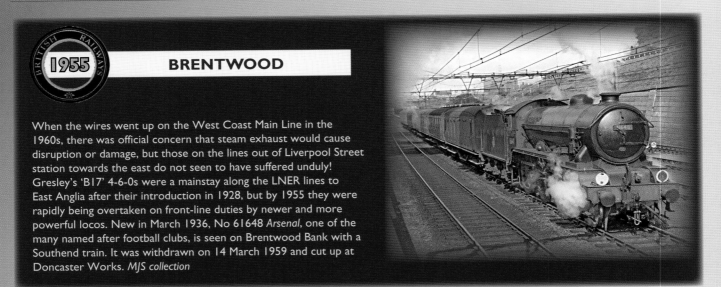

1955 — BRENTWOOD

When the wires went up on the West Coast Main Line in the 1960s, there was official concern that steam exhaust would cause disruption or damage, but those on the lines out of Liverpool Street station towards the east do not seen to have suffered unduly! Gresley's 'B17' 4-6-0s were a mainstay along the LNER lines to East Anglia after their introduction in 1928, but by 1955 they were rapidly being overtaken on front-line duties by newer and more powerful locos. New in March 1936, No 61648 *Arsenal*, one of the many named after football clubs, is seen on Brentwood Bank with a Southend train. It was withdrawn on 14 March 1959 and cut up at Doncaster Works. *MJS collection*

and the spread of overhead wires through Essex, plus the continued delivery of new diesels, brought an end to East Anglian steam by 1962, and, perhaps most dramatically, the appearance of the powerful 'Deltics' swept away the familiar and much-loved sight of Gresley's 'A4s'. Nos D9000 *Royal Scots Grey* and D9001 *St Paddy* were the first to emerge

from English Electric's works, in February 1961, allocated respectively to the Scottish and London ends of the East Coast Main Line (ECML), and their impact was immediate. A further 17 were out on the line by the end of the year and 1961 was to be the last year to see steam on the iconic non-stop 'Elizabethan' express.

Below: In happier times, Doncaster Works built prodigious numbers for the LNER, including Gresley's 'A3s' seen earlier. It also serviced them over the years and two of the class are seen inside the Works in 1963. To the left, No 60044 *Melton* is dappled in sunlight, while No 60108 *Gay Crusader* stands alongside; again, both were named after racehorses. 'Melton' was a thoroughbred horse that won the

Derby in 1885 and was later shipped to Italy for breeding, while 'Gay Crusader' was another thoroughbred. Sired by 'Bayardo' ('A3' No 60079), it won the Triple Crown in 1917 and went on to be featured in a series on Player's cigarette cards. Both locos were withdrawn in 1963 and it is therefore conceivable that this view shows them in for dismantling, rather than repair. *MJS collection*

1963 — DONCASTER

The entire class of 163 Brush Type 2s was allocated to the ER and all were in service by October 1962; they were followed by the end of that year by the first four Brush Type 4s, again allocated to the ER. Thus it was that, surprising to some, the Eastern Region became the first to close to steam, at least over the southern section as far as Peterborough. North of that city, the presence of steam was more sporadic and sheds gradually saw closure – Grantham on 9 September 1963, Lincoln in October 1964 and New England in January 1965. Many of the remaining rosters were for freight and the end finally came at locations such as Doncaster, Frodingham and Immingham in 1966, leaving the North Eastern and Scottish Regions to fly the flag for steam within the ex-LNER grouping.

1955

LONDON (Liverpool Street)

Above: While King's Cross might be regarded as the premier LNER London terminus, at the southern end of the ECML, Liverpool Street was in many ways larger and arguably busier. Another 'B17' 'Footballer' is seen on the turntable at the station in 1955; No 61649 *Sheffield United* is about to be turned before hauling an express from the station. Note the nameplate on the splasher, complete with football and the team's striped colours. New in March 1936, like *Arsenal* seen on the previous page, it was a long-term servant of Ipswich shed and spent the whole of its BR life there. The end came on 14 February 1959, exactly one month prior to *Arsenal*, with a trip north to Doncaster Works for cutting. *MJS collection*

Below: The period covered by this book saw dramatic changes on our railway system, and progress – if that is an appropriate term – seemed and still seems to grow ever faster. Gone are delightful, bucolic views such as this of No 64257 at Basford North station, with a train from Nottingham Victoria in the mid-1950s. Note only does the design of the loco hark back to a previous era, but the rear coaching stock has the same feel, as do the tall elaborate chimneys atop the station building. The smokebox door, too, shows evidence of hard work over time. Introduced by Gresley in 1911, this 0-6-0 class was designated 'J6' by the LNER and rated as 2P3F, indicating that the engines were to be useful as freight locos. However, secondary branch-line duties equally suited them and they carried them out with little fuss. Interestingly, No 64257 is wearing a 38A shedplate, seeming to indicate Colwick shed in Nottingham, but its official depot at this time was 38E (Woodford Halse), having been allocated there from New England in February 1951 and staying there until withdrawal on 16 July 1960. Perhaps it was on loan. *MJS collection*

1955   **BASFORD NORTH**

1964 WORKSOP

Right: The 'B1s', introduced by Thompson in 1942, were the LNER equivalent of the LMS 'Black 5s' – 5MT locomotives that could go anywhere and do almost anything. They were versatile, generally reliable and liked by the crews. Seen at Worksop from a train about to pass on 18 April 1964, No 61120 heads a trio of locos from Retford shed waiting for the road to travel to their respective heavy freight, coal-hauling duties. The other two locos are 2-8-0s Nos 63734 and 63651. A long-term resident of Doncaster shed, this 'B1' moved to Retford in November 1959 and stayed there until its demise on 6 February 1965. *Ray Ruffell, Silver Link collection*

Right: On the day of a visit to Mexborough shed on 14 June 1964, this 'B1' was the only loco present, but all is not what it seems. No 61050 is not withdrawn, but merely utilising the availability of the wheeldrop at the shed; it went on to serve another 13 months before withdrawal. Much of its early existence was in and around Norwich before a move to Sheffield in 1956. Thereafter there were various moves until the end at Langwith Junction on 17 July 1965. Replacing the two earlier engine sheds (opened in 1847 and 1854) closer to Mexborough station, this newer facility opened its doors in 1875, with 12 roads, massively expanding on the previous space. It also sat alongside an equal number of sidings. It closed four months prior to this view and was later demolished. *MJS*

1964 MEXBOROUGH

1964

DONCASTER

Right: The final year of the first decade of the 21st century saw the emergence of No 60163 *Tornado*, the first main-line steam engine to be built in this country since 1960 (see later in this book). It is a replica of Peppercorn's Class 'A1', a development of Thompson's 'A1/1' introduced in 1945. One of BR's 'A1s', No 60141 *Abbotsford*, stands in Doncaster shed yard on 14 June 1964. Several of the class had names connected with Sir Walter Scott; Abbotsford House, on the south bank of the River Tweed near Galashiels, was within the estate that he acquired in 1811. He built and extended the property and took residence in 1824; it was then in his family's ownership until his last descendent died in 2004. *MJS*

Below: The fourth class of 4-6-2 express locomotives for the LNER - the 'A2s' – was introduced in 1943, when Thompson rebuilt Gresley's Class 'P2' 2-8-2. Comprising a number of variants, the class finally numbered 40 and, although well-liked by enthusiasts, they were not as successful as Gresley's earlier designs. On 9 July 1956 No 60508 *Duke of Rothesay* roars past Retford South signal box and over the flat and diamond crossings on its way from King's Cross. The loco's name was the title of the heir apparent to the Kingdom of Scotland prior to 1707, to Great Britain from 1707 to 1801, and the United Kingdom thereafter. The present incumbent is, of course, HRH Prince Charles. The second 'new-build' 'A2', fitted with large smoke deflectors in January 1947, it was a one-shed loco for many years up to its end, being withdrawn from New England on 11 March 1961, one of the later ones to be dispensed with from those early examples. *MJS collection*

1956

RETFORD

Right: Those fortunate enough to have witnessed the grandeur that was Nottingham Victoria station will remember its magnificence and majestic nature. The sheer scale of the excavations to create the space in which it was built is clear from this view of No 61826 passing the North signal box as it enters with a local from the north. Designed by Albert Edward Lambert for the GCR and GNR, the station was opened by the Nottingham Joint Station Committee on 24 May 1900 and handled many important express services well into the 1950s, such as 'The South Yorkshireman' and 'The Master Cutler', as well as a myriad of local services and freight trains, fast and slow. Following the decision to close the through route to Marylebone, then the remaining DMU service from Rugby, the doors finally closed on 4 September 1967. Demolition followed, against much vociferous local opposition, leaving just the station's original clock tower within the present Victoria Shopping Centre. *MJS collection*

1957   NOTTINGHAM (Victoria)

Right: Canklow shed – which once employed one John Prescott – also opened in 1900, replacing an earlier facility at Rotherham Masbrough station. A square brick roundhouse with one through road, it closed on 11 October 1965, remaining in use as a factory until demolition in the 1980s. Originally a Midland Railway shed, it was transferred to the Eastern Region in the 1950s but still kept its association with its former owners by virtue of housing largely ex-LMS locos. One such, on a regular roster from Burton-on-Trent, is 'Jubilee' No 45620 *North Borneo*, sadly devoid of nameplate, on 14 June 1964. Inside on that day was another Burton-on-Trent 'Jubilee', evidence of the volume of traffic between the two locations. Withdrawal was on 3 October and cutting was swift, at Cashmore's, Great Bridge, in January 1965. *MJS*

1964   CANKLOW

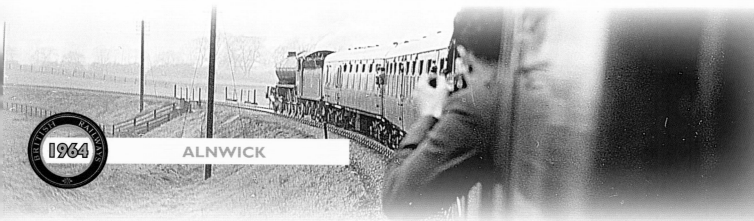

1964 ALNWICK

1964 ALNWICK

Compared to the Eastern Region, BR(NE) was a much smaller entity, more tightly encapsulated within boundaries, especially in the early days of British Railways, stretching from Leeds (in the south-west) and Hull (south-east) to Berwick in the north, through Darlington and Newcastle along the way and describing a long vertical triangle, progressively narrowing to a pinnacle at its northernmost tip. Just three tentacles stretched westwards – Northallerton to Hawes, Darlington to Tebay, and Newcastle to Carlisle – as the old NER tried to insinuate its presence and influence into 'enemy' territory. Within this triangle, the Region had a full gamut of services and locomotive duties, from express passenger to local and commuter, and to short- and long-distance freight. The terrain in many parts was distinctly contrary to easy running, so locomotives perforce had to have stamina and inherent power, especially for the cross-country 'tentacle' routes and the heavy ore and coal trains.

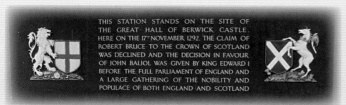

THIS STATION STANDS ON THE SITE OF THE GREAT HALL OF BERWICK CASTLE. HERE ON THE 17ᵗʰ NOVEMBER 1292. THE CLAIM OF ROBERT BRUCE TO THE CROWN OF SCOTLAND WAS DECLINED AND THE DECISION IN FAVOUR OF JOHN BALIOL WAS GIVEN BY KING EDWARD I BEFORE THE FULL PARLIAMENT OF ENGLAND AND A LARGE GATHERING OF THE NOBILITY AND POPULACE OF BOTH ENGLAND AND SCOTLAND

Top: Travelling by train has always been popular, and over the years rail tours specifically geared to either enthusiasts or the general public have remained great attractions. One of past joys, not so easily available in modern rolling stock and frowned upon by authorities, was to lean from carriage windows to catch glimpses of the train. On 25 April 1964 our intrepid photographer captures No 61435 as it pulls away from Northallerton, heading the RCTS (West Riding Branch) 'North Yorkshireman Rail Tour', originating from Leeds City. *Ray Ruffell, Silver Link collection*

Above: The sign that greets travellers as they descend the steps to Berwick's station, seen on 1 July 1989. *Ray Ruffell, Silver Link collection*

Above: Although on a through route from Alnmouth to Coldstream in Northumberland, Alnwick operated as a terminus, requiring through trains to reverse. The sturdy stone walls supporting the overall wooden trainshed led to a gloom within the station that is magnified by the late afternoon shadows of 3 February 1964, as No 62012 simmers before resuming its journey. *Ray Ruffell, Silver Link collection*

At the birth of British Railways in 1948, the Region inherited 32 'main' sheds, many with sub-sheds allotted to them, having responsibility for around 1,900 engines. Perhaps not surprisingly, in view of its strategic position both within the Region and also on the ECML – and having two distinct shed locations, north and south of the station – York enjoyed the largest allocation, with, also perhaps not expectedly, Hull (Dairycoates) not far behind. Indeed, the total gracing the three individual sheds within Hull was about 15% of the whole Region's operational fleet – although that was to change in 1956 as will be seen below. Elsewhere, Heaton, Darlington and Newport all had allocations in excess of 100.

There were a number of boundary changes during BR's tenure of our railways, and three that were to have a major impact on the operational duties and character of the North Eastern Region took place between July 1956 and February 1957. The first saw the ex-LNER Leeds area sheds at Ardsley, Copley Hill and Bradford (Hammerton Street) come under Wakefield's control; next, the ex-LMS Wakefield 25A area sheds – including Goole, Mirfield, Sowerby Bridge, Low Moor and Farnley Junction – were split between Wakefield, Hull and Leeds control; and finally, the five ex-LMS Leeds area sheds moved, en bloc, to the North Eastern. All were consequently given appropriate BR(NE) codes and although their locations did nothing to alter the shape of the Region, as they were all cheek-by-jowl with their erstwhile competitors, the moves did change the face of the duties undertaken, not least with the addition to the Region of Holbeck and Neville Hill sheds.

Below: In steam days, the northern exit from Newcastle-upon-Tyne station was sharply divergent, creating a myriad of lines and several diamond crossings. Photographs from the castle, in the background, are well-known and show the potential for conflict with alarming clarity. This view, from the ground and looking north, shows the main ECML route swinging to the left, and to the right the tracks over the High Level Bridge to Gateshead. This bridge can just be glimpsed in the far right distance, with a Metro-Cammell two-car DMU having just crossed the Tyne and approaching Central station. In the foreground, on 3 February 1964, No 67684 approaches light engine, to run through the platform and take up its role as station pilot. *Ray Ruffell, Silver Link collection*

1964   NEWCASTLE UPON TYNE

In line with other regions, withdrawal of branch lines and/or local stations and services led to reduction in locomotive numbers, with, again, the older types being the first to feel the effect. New engines were also appearing on many of the freight duties, not least the powerful BR 9F 2-10-0s on duties such as the iron-ore trains out of Consett. Seven were introduced from November 1955 – Nos 92060-66 – all allocated to Tyne Dock shed and purpose-fitted with Westinghouse-type air-pumps to operate the iron-ore hoppers to the steelworks at Consett, 1,000 feet above sea level, which included a section at 1 in 35 in places. They were all finally withdrawn between 1965 and 1967.

1958 onwards saw a gradual but progressive closure of sheds – beginning with Newport and Middlesbrough, with the opening of a new facility at Thornaby – bringing about reductions

Above: When most trains were loco-hauled, as opposed to the norm in the 21st century of trains formed of self-powered units of various types, a standby was provided at strategic points in case of failure. Late on 29 August 1964, with the sun about to drop behind the clouds in the west, No 60036 *Colombo* is in light steam at Darlington shed ready for just such an eventuality. Allocated to Leeds (Neville Hill) shed for many years, it finally left there in June 1961, to travel across Leeds to Copley Hill, then, three months later, another short trip, to Ardsley. June 1963 saw it at Gateshead shed, before another move after six months to Darlington. It was withdrawn on 28 November 1964. Another one to be despatched quickly, it moved a relatively short distance, compared to many others, to A. Draper & Sons Ltd in Hull in January 1965. *MJS*

Right: This sign is from Levisham, on the North Yorkshire Moors Railway.

NORTH EASTERN RAILWAY
PUBLIC WARNING
PERSONS ARE WARNED NOT TO TRESPASS ON THIS RAILWAY, OR ON ANY OF THE LINES, STATIONS, WORKS, OR PREMISES CONNECTED THEREWITH.
ANY PERSON SO TRESPASSING IS LIABLE TO A PENALTY OF FORTY SHILLINGS.
SECRETARY.

1964

GATESHEAD

in stock as the spread of dieselisation, road competition and changes in traffic practices took their toll. Thus it was that the area fought a rearguard action, especially with the freight workings, and it is ironic that the part of the country that 'invented' the railway – for just

such traffic 140 years earlier – should be among the last in the UK to dispense with steam, surviving past all bar the area across the Pennines, to finally see the final end in the latter months of 1967, with Holbeck closing to steam on 1 December.

1967

WAKEFIELD

Top: With its 'enemy' right behind and the condition of the smokebox door pointing to possible problems inside, it is fairly obvious that No 60040 *Cameronian* is unlikely to work again; indeed, on 29 August 1964 it has puffed its last, having been withdrawn on 25 July. Finally allocated to Gateshead, where it is seen at the side of the shed, it had enjoyed a yo-yo existence for the whole of its BR life, oscillating between Gateshead and Darlington, with just one short six-month deviation, to Heaton, between December 1962 and June 1963. It also enjoyed a brief spell in blue livery in 1951. The final cut came at Hughes Bolckow Ltd, Blyth, within a month of this view. *Les Wade, MJS collection*

Left: Vividly demonstrating the appalling condition that many of the surviving locomotives were in towards the end of steam, No 42269 stands forlorn at Wakefield on 9 April 1967. One of a class of 2-6-4Ts introduced by Fairburn as a 1945 development of Stanier's earlier design, it was once a proud servant of Scottish depots, sharing space in Edinburgh, Aviemore, Dumfries and Glasgow, before emigrating south to Wakefield in October 1964. With a rope around the chimney, its dented tank and general dismal appearance, it would seem to have been discarded already, but in fact it was not officially put to one side until 15 July 1967. *MJS collection*

1957 LEICESTER (Belgrave Road)

1955 CRAVEN ARMS (LM)

Created in 1948 from the old LMS system, the London Midland Region – BR(M) – was by far the largest part of British Railways, with tentacles stretching out in many directions. From Swansea (Victoria) in deepest south-west Wales, through Bath (Green Park) to Broadstone Junction almost on the South Coast, via Cheltenham to Andover, Fenchurch Street to Shoeburyness, Bedford to Hitchin, Kettering to Huntingdon, Stamford to Peterborough, Nottingham to Lincoln, Knottingley to Goole, and with influence in Scotland – all these routes, either under direct or shared control – were part of the empire in addition to the great swathe of land inhabited by the two main lines out of Euston and St Pancras, through to Carlisle and the Scottish

Top left: Though at the end of a long branch passing through sparsely populated countryside, the GNR wanted its incursion into 'enemy territory' not to be overlooked and built a grand Victorian edifice at Leicester (Belgrave Road) that was always far too large for the traffic available. It saw a slow and gradual decline in passenger services; indeed, all bar seasonal holiday traffic and occasional workmen's trains had ceased by the time of this view in June 1957. Long-preserved ex-Midland Railway Nos 118 and 158A stand under the massive trainshed during the 'Leicester & Midland Railway Centenary Exhibition', the admission to which was 6d for adults and 3d for children! *Doug Giles, MJS collection*

Above: We have already seen on page 21 an ex-GWR loco in store at Craven Arms shed, but here, on 11 April 1955, we have two ancient ex-LMS types. Nos 58904 and 58207 are ragged and awaiting disposal at the side of the shed building. Craven Arms was a sub-shed of Shrewsbury and both locos ended their days here officially on 13 August 1955, although as can be seen their working lives have already ended. No 58904 was one of Webb's 'Coal Tank' 0-6-2Ts, originally introduced in 1882; although archaic compared to its neighbour, No 58207's class design was actually the older, coming from Johnson's introduction in 1875. *Gerald Adams, MJS collection*

Left: Like other regions, BR's Midland Region used elderly locos for works shunting. At Horwich use was made of some of Aspinall's 1891 rebuilds of Barton Wright's 0-6-0s from 1877, which were still extant at Nationalisation. Retaining their ex-LMS numbers, although officially given BR numbers, in this case 51305, they served for many years. Seen on 9 February 1964 in very dull weather conditions, No 11305 was the last of the class to be withdrawn, on Boxing Day 1964. *MJS*

1964 HORWICH

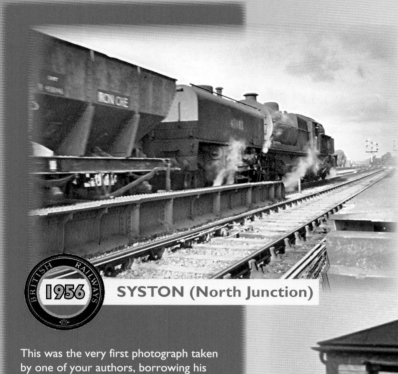

1956 **SYSTON (North Junction)**

border. Of the total steam fleet inherited by BR in 1948, BR(M) had not far short of 40% - in excess of 7,800 locomotives.

While pre-BR steam locomotive designs continued to be built, as elsewhere, some of these new Midland Region engines were somewhat more catholic in their places of work than their contemporaries. For example, Nos 41240-41243 (new in October/December 1949) went straight to Southern Region-coded Bath (Green Park); 41290-41319 (October 1951-June 1952) all went to the SR; 42055-42060 (November/December 1950) to the Scottish Region; and 42066-42106 (between February 1950 and August 1952 – not in strict order) to the SR.

This was the very first photograph taken by one of your authors, borrowing his father's camera. Travelling between Syston and Loughborough on his way to and from school from September 1954, the sight of freights nose-to-tail on the slow lines behind, in the main, Stanier 8Fs and 'Garratts', was something to truly savour; thus the opportunity to snap No 47982, heading north from Syston North Junction on 1 June 1956, was one not to be missed. These mighty beasts were sorely missed when they began to disappear from the mid-1950s, and this example succumbed to the inevitable on 28 December 1957, the last but one of the class to go. *MJS*

Main picture: Tewkesbury had two stations over time, the first in the centre of the town and the other on the outskirts. The former, opened in 1840 and horse-worked from Ashchurch for the first four years, served both the town and a local mill. Graced with an engine shed into the steam era, it was replaced by the second facility when the branch from Ashchurch was extended to Great Malvern in the 1860s. This latter location is seen towards the end – passenger services ceased on 14 August 1961 – with the slightly grander station building installed in 1872 to the right. Ex-LMS 3F 0-6-0 No 43754 was a regular on the branch and lingered on at Gloucester (Barnwood) shed until the early part of 1963. Note the interest of the youngsters on the platform. *MJS*

Akin to other regions, much of the stock inherited was decidedly elderly, and many of the more than 100 classes had just one member or a small handful. By 1955 this number had been dramatically reduced by around a third, but still around at the beginning of our period was the famed 'Big Bertha', No 58100, built in 1919 for banking the Lickey Incline, and the 33 LMS 'Garratts', built by Beyer Peacock & Co between 1927 and 1930, the only main-line examples of this type in the UK, apart from the sole LNER engine. Many of the veteran types also survived, managing to find regular work. Sadly 'Bertha' was withdrawn from Bromsgrove shed on 19 May 1956 and consigned to history. 1955 saw seven of the 2-6-6-2T 'Garratts' discarded, with their role on the Toton-Brent coal trains being invaded by both Stanier 8Fs and the newly introduced 'Standard' 9Fs, and the whole class disappeared when the last member, No 47994, was officially put aside at Hasland shed on 19 April 1958.

The cull of old and then not-so-old steam on the Region was initially slow and protracted – only a little in excess of 10% over the seven years to the beginning of 1955 – but, again like other areas, this was to begin to change more dramatically as the years passed and the 'switching' of sheds between regions already seen had little impact on the overall total in operation. The numbers were slightly bolstered by the addition of new

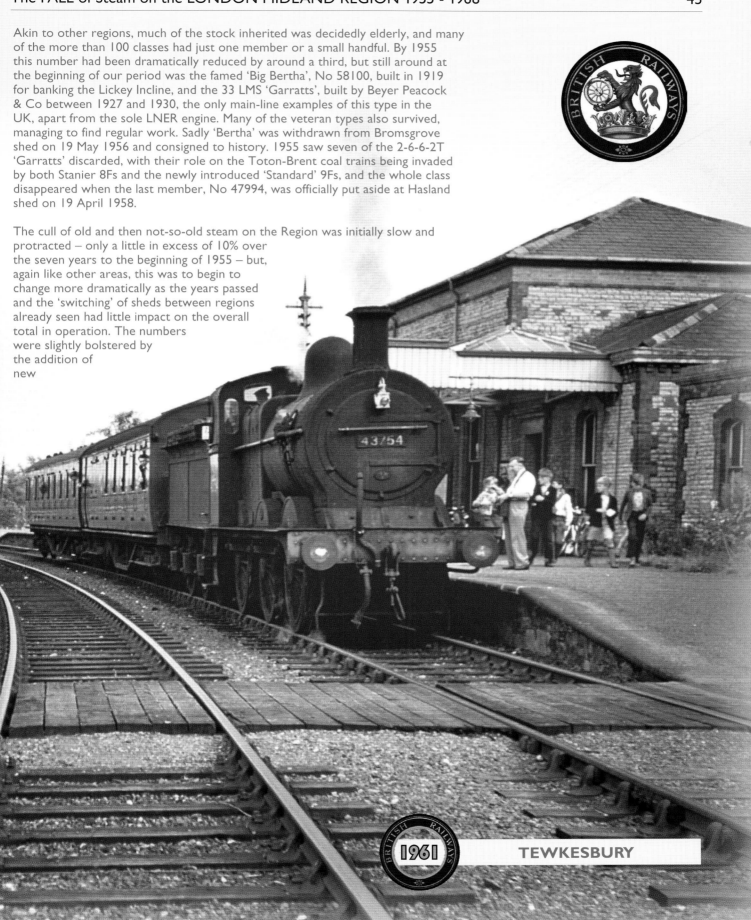

1961   TEWKESBURY

1957   CAMDEN BANK

One of the most powerful locomotives designed and built by BR – second only to the later 9F 2-10-0s – and originally designed to take the place of the WCML 'flagship' 'Duchesses', was No 71000 *Duke of Gloucester*, new to Crewe North depot on 19 June 1954. Five months later it had six months of trials from Swindon shed before coming back to its home at Crewe, where it stayed until the end on 1 December 1962. Eight and a half years was a criminally short lifespan, but the uniqueness of the design and some of the initiatives incorporated within it proved its downfall, together with the onslaught of dieselisation and ultimately electrification of its route. Some of the might and power of the engine can be judged from this view of it storming out of Euston, up Camden Bank, in May 1957 with its ten-coach northbound express. *MJS collection*

builds, with one being of particular interest. Introduced in 1954 and built at Derby, No 71000 *Duke of Gloucester,* though slightly lighter and with reduced tractive effort compared to the LMS 'Pacifics', was meant to be something approaching a modern, 'state-of-the-art' express engine, but sadly things did not quite work out that way. A further 21% on the books had gone over the next five years, to the turn of the next decade, when dieselisation then electrification would make ever greater incursions into steam's stronghold.

On 2 March 1959 a complete system, rather than a branch or stretch of line, suffered withdrawal, when the Leicester (London Road)-Yarmouth (Beach) through route – one of the LMS's 'joint' operations – was closed to passengers. Kettering-Huntingdon followed on 15 June and subsequent years progressed the trend. The contraction of the steam fleet inevitably followed, with a further 57% reduction between the beginning of 1960 and 1965, leaving just over 2,300 locomotives still in action.

1962　DURSLEY

The LMS branch to Dursley, Gloucestershire, struck due south from the Bristol-Birmingham main line at Coaley Junction, with just one station en route, at Cam. The terminus was squeezed between industrial sites and the tightness of this final stretch is apparent as No 43593 stands with its short train on 10 September 1962, the very last day of passenger workings. Neither Cam nor Dursley were areas of large population for much of the branch's life, and although the industrial units did provide freight traffic, it can hardly have ever been really cost-effective as a branch line. Goods traffic battled on until 13 July 1970, after which the line was dispensed with and lifted. The junction station was also closed and, more recently, a facility for Cam has been opened on the main line, roughly a quarter of a mile north-east, towards Stonehouse. No 43593 did very little work after leaving the branch until its end three months later. *Gerald Adams, MJS collection*

1960 RUGBY

Rugby (Midland) station was a Mecca for enthusiasts, with branches coming in from all points of the compass and the former GCR line crossing the WCML just south of the station. There was also the presence of an engine shed with a useful allocation, and the LMS Testing Station within its grounds. While many locomotive types could be somewhat parochial, there were other types that wandered far and wide, giving spotters the hope of seeing a rare 'cop'. One such on this day was a real delight for your photographer, as 'Jubilee' No 45705 *Seahorse* heads south for Euston on 22 May 1960, with a special working from Blackpool. Once at Leeds, it was a resident at the West Coast seaside town for eight years from June 1956 until a move to Newton Heath, Manchester, and finally withdrawal on 6 November 1965. It was cut at Cashmore's Great Bridge scrapyard the following month. *MJS*

1965 LEICESTER (MIDLAND)

1963   **RUDDINGTON**

Opposite: There are numerous places throughout the UK where the railway scene and its surroundings have seen dramatic changes. In this view overlooking Leicester (Midland) shed in October 1965, the low squat building to the right of centre is the only structure still extant in the 21st century – everything else, in and beyond the railway land, has disappeared, and even this view is now obscured by tree growth over the past decade or so. Many of the actual tracks remain in situ, but they are now rusted through non-use. Once enjoying an allocation in excess of 70, the shed closed to steam officially on 13 June 1965 but, as can be seen, it is still in use four months later. The roundhouse was demolished in 1970. *MJS*

Above: One of the ambitions and proud boasts of the preserved Great Central Railway is the recreation of the 'Windcutter' trains, rakes of mineral wagons hauled at speed by 'Standard' 9F 2-10-0s. While this recreation is impressive and aesthetically appealing for today's visitors to the line, it cannot have the authenticity as shown here, of the 9F looking hard-worked and careworn. On an unidentified date, but thought to be around 1963, No 92011 heads south through Ruddington. New in May 1954, it first worked in East Anglia before moving to Annesley, on the outskirts of Nottingham, in June 1957. Thereafter it was a solid and reliable servant of the GC route, often working south through Leicester, until a further change of district came, to Birkenhead, in August 1965. Withdrawal came on 2 December 1967, just eight months prior to the end of steam on BR. *MJS collection*

The latter year saw the remaining stock ever more concentrated, as many erstwhile active steam depots shed their servants, such as Willesden (from 27 September), Watford (29 March), Rugby (25 May), Crewe North (24 May), Bangor and Kettering (14 June), and Bushbury and Bury (12 April). The combination of line closures, dieselisation and electrification and the perpetual competition from road transport led to further transformation over the ensuing couple of years leading to, by the closing of the summer of 1967, the effective end of steam everywhere except the North West of England.

1960 Nr GRANGE-OVER-SANDS

Left: Holiday locations were often sources of new and sometimes exotic locomotives, and for any spotter trips to places far away were certainly to be eagerly anticipated. The Cumbrian Coast route, from Carnforth to Carlisle via Barrow-in-Furness, was an area not visited by everyone, so the delights were many and varied for the lucky enthusiast. Grange-over-Sands is seen on 28 August 1960, as 'Jubilee' No 45726 *Vindictive* passes the edges of Morecambe Bay on its way to Barrow.

Below: Later the same day we are on the platform at Grange, to witness No 42119 arriving with what will be the 5.40pm Sunday-only service to Barrow. Despite its resemblance to earlier LMS designs, this loco was actually a BR product, being new on 8 October 1949. Initially at Watford, at the southern end of the WCML, it gradually made its way north, via Stoke in 1954, Wigan in 1957, and Barrow from June 1959. It officially finally expired on 11 September 1965. *Both Ray Ruffell, Silver Link collection*

So, by the turn of 1968 just 12 sheds still had steam (listed with their final codings): Edge Hill (8A), Speke Junction (8C), Northwich (8E), Stockport (Edgeley) (9B), Trafford Park (9E), Heaton Mersey (9F), Rose Grove (10F), Lostock Hall (10D), Carnforth (10A), Newton Heath (9D), Bolton (9K) and Patricroft (9H). These accommodated around 350 engines in the Liverpool, Manchester and mid/north Lancashire areas. As the year went on, even these were progressively culled and enthusiasts were forced to travel ever wider to obtain their latest steam fix. Thus the end came, many years earlier than had originally been planned, formally on 4

1960 GRANGE-OVER-SANDS

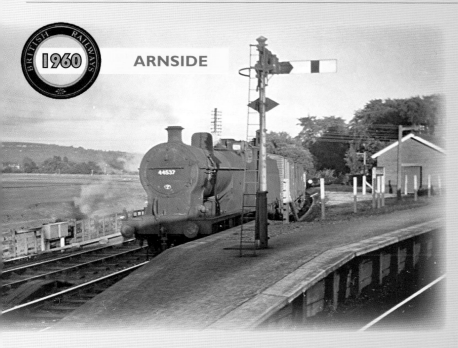

1960 ARNSIDE

Left: Arnside was the stop before Grange on the route from Carnforth, and was also a junction for a short branch to the WCML at Hincaster Junction. The northern stretch, from Sandside to Hincaster, was closed on 9 September 1963, with the short stub remaining to Arnside succumbing on 1 January 1972. In slightly happier times, on 25 August 1960, No 44537 has shunted its heavy freight wagons onto this branch, to allow the passage of the Carnforth-Barrow train on which the photographer is travelling. Having been delayed by the freight, the driver of the passenger train apparently gave his colleague on the 4F his thoughts on the matter, in rather colourful language!

Below: As with other parts of the UK, the end of steam did not come in one fell swoop, but was often overtaken by stealth. With diesel units having replaced much of the local traffic on the former Maryport & Carlisle route through Cumbria, the sole remaining steam presence was the 3.25pm Saturdays-only Carlisle-Workington train. It is seen here on 27 August 1960 with No 46455 prepared and ready for the off. Another continuation of an LMS type by BR, it was new in May 1950, going first to Penrith. It then stayed there or at Workington until a transfer to Carlisle in January 1960. Withdrawal was on 20 May 1967 and it was cut up at McWilliams's Shettleston site the following October. *Both Ray Ruffell, Silver Link collection*

August 1968, with hundreds of spotters descending on the area. Apart from one or two 'rogue' workings, where, perhaps, steam had rescued a diesel, and the famous 'Fifteen Guinea Special' on 11 August, the curtain came down and the final iron horse had been corralled behind closed doors with the future decidedly bleak. Happily, some did escape the cutter's torch and together, with more luck than judgement buying time, they found their way to new and safer homes, which story is told later in this volume.

1960 CARLISLE

21st July 1968 Roch Valley Railway Society	
Locos Used	44888, 45110 & 70013 *Oliver Cromwell*
Stock Used	8x coaches (BSK, 6x BSO, BSK)
Route :	**1T40 throughout**
Loco	Route
44888	Manchester Victoria - Newton le Willows - Earelstown - Broad Green - Olive Mount - Edge Lane - Bootle Jn - Southport avoiding curve
70013	Southport avoiding curve - Meols Cop - Wigan Wallgate - Crows Nest Jn - Bolton - Clifton Jn - Windsor Bridge No.3 - Manchester Victoria - Cheetham Hill - Rochdale - Todmorden - Copy Pit - Rose Grove - Blackburn - Lostock Hall - Moss Lane - Burscough North Jn - Burscough Bridge - Meols Cop - Southport Chapel Street
45110	Southport Chapel Street - Meols Cop - Burscough Bridge - Burscough South Jn - Ormskirk - Aintree Cheshire Lines Jn - Aintree Central - Fazakerley South Jn - Old Swan & Knotty Ash - Halewood North Jn - Halewood East Jn - Hough Green - Widnes East - Warrington Central - Manchester Central
Notes :	
(1) The purpose of this tour was to do Manchester to Southport four different ways.	

Timings (Booked & Actual)		
Location	Booked	Actual
Manchester Victoria	10.22d	10.52
Deal Street	10/24	?
Cross Lane	10/29	?
Barton Moss	10/34	?
Kenyon Jn	10/42	?
Earlestown	10/51	?
St Helens Junction	10/55	?
Huyton	11/03	11/40
Broad Green	11/07	?
Olive Mount	11/10	?
Edge Lane	11/16	?
Bootle Jn	11/29	12/09
Bootle Oriel Road	11c30 ~ 11c32	12.10 ~ 12.11
Marsh Lane Jn	11/34	?
Hall Road	11/43	12/21
Southport	12L00a ~ 12L10d	?
Southport curve	?	??L?? ~ 12L57
St Lukes	12/13	13.00a ~ ??.??d
Meols Cop	12/16	?
Burscough Bridge	12/24	?
Wigan Wallgate	12/36	?
Hindley No.2	12/39	?
Crow Nest	12/41	13/30
Lostock Jn	12/50	?
Bolton	12/55	13/40
Clifton Jn	13/04	13/49
Windsor Bridge No.3	13/08	?

Manchester Victoria	13.13a ~ 13.45d	??.?? ~ 14.10
Footbridge	13/47	?
Cheetham Hill	13/49	14/19
Newton Heath	13/53	?
Castleton East Jn	14/02	?
Rochdale	14.05a ~ 14.07d	14.45 ~ 14.46
Todmorden	14/20	15/01
Stansfield Hall	14/23	?
Copy Pit	14/33	15/10
Rose Grove (shed visit)	14.43a ~ 15.21d	15.18 ~ 15.37
Accrington	15/31	15/46
Blackburn	15/41	15/53
Bamber Bridge	15/53	16/03
Lostock Hall (shed visit)	15.55a ~ 16.25d	??.?? ~ 16.32
Moss Lane	16/28	16/35
Burscough North Jn	16/40	16/47
Burscough Bridge	16/42	16/48
Meols Cop	16/50	?
St Lukes	16/52	16/56

Southport	16L55a ~ 17L23d	16.59 ~ 17.22
Meols Cop	17/28	17/26
Burscough Bridge	17/37	17/36
Burscough Jn	17/40	?
Ormskirk	17/44	17/42
Aintree Cheshire Lines Jn	17/54	17/53
Aintree Central	17/57	17/54
Fazakerley	18/02	?
Halewood North	18/12	18/12
Halewood East Jn	18/15	18/13
Hough Green	18.20a ~ 18.30d	18.17 ~ 18.29
Widnes East	18/35	?
Sankey Jn	18/38	18/41
Warrington Central	18/40	18/43
Padgate Jn	18/42	18/46
Glazebrook East Jn	18/47	18/51
Trafford Park Jn	18/56	?
Manchester Central	19.01a	19.04

Information courtesy of:
Six Bells Junction (www.sixbellsjunction.co.uk)
Sources : David Hills (compiled from contemporary reports), Chris Totty & Kevin Driscoll

1968 GLAZEBROOK (East Junction)

1962 **LONDON (St Pancras)**

Right: St Pancras station has had an eventful and sometimes chequered history, but has now been transformed almost beyond recognition into the terminus for HS1 from the Channel Tunnel, with 'Javelins' and 'Eurostars' the exotic presence. In more mundane steam days it was beloved by enthusiasts and photographers, and both are combined in this view of No 45285, at 11.02am on 20 January 1962, waiting to head north out of the station confines. A long-term London resident – at Kentish Town and Cricklewood sheds, serving the latter on this date – it gradually moved north, with time at Derby, Llandudno Junction, Crewe and Carlisle before withdrawal on 30 December 1967. *MJS collection*

Below: The shadows are long and low as No 44733 lets off steam as it stands in the platform at Preston station on 25 August 1960. Parcels are being loaded into the front coach and the crew watch from their cab, ready for the off when they have the road, with a train bound for Blackpool. *Ray Ruffell, Silver Link collection*

1960 **PRESTON**

1953

FORT WILLIAM

Top: Situated close to Ben Nevis, Fort William station is an obvious destination for travellers. The lure of steam on this West Highland, ex-North British Railway, route was obvious in earlier times and has remained into the 21st century, with enterprising rail tour operators taking the necessary steps. Though slightly earlier than the scope of this volume, 'Black 5' No 44975 is the real thing as it stands at the buffer stop in 1953. This being a terminus, the train will need to reverse for the continuation of the journey to Mallaig. The loco is on Perth's books at this date, but would move to Fort William's own shed late in the following year, before its final journey to Dalry Road (Edinburgh) shed until 25 September 1965. *Doug Giles, MJS collection*

1954

BLAIRGOWRIE

Above: Blairgowrie was the terminus for the short Caledonian Railway branch from Coupar Angus, on the route between Perth and Forfar. Despite being equipped with just one platform face, it was graced with an overall trainshed roof and a long and wide platform, to accommodate the normal two-coach branch train! On 14 August 1954 No 55169 has arrived from Dundee (West) via Alyth Junction, less than five months from closure on 10 January 1955. *Peter Hay, Silver link collection*

The creation of the Scottish Region was the first attempt at forming a self-contained railway system within the country's borders. Prior to 1948, both the LMS and the LNER held the reins of operation, with locomotives beginning with '4' or '5' (ex-LMS) and '6' (ex-LNER); in addition, two ex-GWR-style 0-6-0PTs, Nos 1646 (February 1957-February 1963) and 1649 (July 1958-February 1963), were allocated to Helmsdale for work on the Dornoch branch!

Historically, the country's highlands and lowlands were explored by the Glasgow & South Western, Caledonian, North British, Highland and Great North of Scotland railways, with much criss-crossing of lines in places, as rival companies fought for traffic and dominance.

At Nationalisation, the legacy of these old railways still endured, with both the LMS and the LNER sharing examples of ancient types. With the topography of the railway system, not least with long stretches through isolated countryside and over tortuous terrain, in addition to the more intense passenger duties in and around Glasgow and Edinburgh, locomotives tended to be designed for need more than elsewhere in the UK. Good examples of this were Gresley's 'K4' 2-6-0s, three-cylinder engines with 5ft 2in driving wheels to cope with the challenges of the switchback nature of the West Highland Line; James Johnson's 'D41' and Pickersgill's 'D40' 4-4-0s for the GNoSR; and Reid's 'D29' and the derivative 'D30', plus the 'D34' 4-4-0s, for

1958 **HELMSDALE**

Above: It is 15 June 1958 and the summer sun shines brightly on the immaculately turned out No 54495 at Helmsdale shed, receiving some casual attention before its next trip out. Apart from Thurso and Wick, Helmsdale was the most northerly of engine sheds, coded 60C (under the overall umbrella of Inverness) and with sub-sheds at Dornoch and Tain. Originally a two-road dead-end shed opened on 19 June 1871, it was replaced on the same site in 1899. After a gale demolished this in 1921, another structure was built, again on the same site, with a Dutch-barn-style roof, and a 55-foot turntable to replace the earlier 40-foot (later 50-foot) version. It closed in July 1961 and was subsequently demolished. One of Pickersgill's 3P '72' Class 4-4-0s of 1920, No 54495 was a stalwart of Helmsdale shed for many years up to its eventual demise on 24 March 1962, an attractive but antiquated design surviving into the diesel era! Note the open, somewhat barren but very attractive backdrop. *MJS collection*

Left: Many of the Scottish stations inherited names redolent of drama, majesty and a hint of mystery, and Ballindalloch, on the Great North of Scotland branch from Boat of Garten to Craigellachie, was no exception. Many of the locos employed in Scotland never came south of the border and, as such, were intriguing and beguiling to 'Sassenach' spotters! Humdrum, yet superbly suitable in design for the duties asked of them, members of McIntosh's '812' Class 0-6-0s still had great appeal, the power and honesty being amply displayed in this view of No 57591 rounding the curve into the station on 12 August 1955 with a rake of box vans. A long-time resident of Inverness shed, it officially left there in 1954, but here still wears the now inappropriate 60A shedplate. *Silver Link collection*

1955 **BALLINDALLOCH**

Left: Perhaps not surprisingly, in view of its size and strategic importance geographically, there are myriads of lines in and around Edinburgh. A cat's cradle of routes was developed by the conflicting aspirations of the Caledonian and North British railways, and the area around Leith, north of Waverley station on the banks of the Firth of Forth, was particularly well served. Sadly, however, the onset and development of bus services wreaked havoc with both tram and train services locally, and even the introduction of DMUs could not make the NB line to North Leith economical. On 7 April 1958, just a month before the takeover, the fireman of the 1.43pm train to Edinburgh (Princes Street) looks back forlornly for one or two more passengers to join the mere handful already on the train. No 57559, wearing the 64C shedplate of Dalry Road (Edinburgh) shed, was a veteran of that shed and stayed there until the end for it on 21 October 1961. *Silver Link collection*

Below: In the period under investigation in this section, the Caledonian route west through Argyll split at Connel Ferry, on the shores of Loch Etive, going north to Ballachulish and south to Oban. The former ceased handling goods traffic on 1 June 1965 and closed

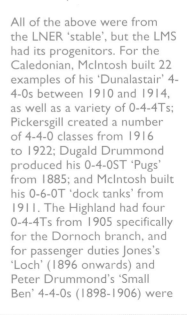

NORTH LEITH — 1958

completely on 28 March the following year, but the much shorter stretch to Oban remains open today, taking some 3 hours from Glasgow. In this delightful view, from April 1958, the crew of No 55263 discuss some matter with the Guard, while a small group of businessmen enjoy the spring sunshine for a few moments more before taking their seats. The loco was another of those in Scotland that spent many years operating from just one depot, in this case Oban itself. *Silver Link collection*

OBAN — 1958

the North British. Later innovations for work north of the border were the post-Grouping 'D11/2' 4-4-0s – introduced in 1924 to fit the Scottish loading gauge and derived from Robinson's 1920-designed 'Large Directors' – and Peppercorn's 1945 adaptation of Thompson's rebuilding of Gresley's 'K4' No 61997 *MacCailin Mor*, classified as 'K1'. Happily, examples of both the 'K1' and 'K4' survive in preservation, as BR Nos 62005 and 61994 *The Great Marquess*.

All of the above were from the LNER 'stable', but the LMS had its progenitors. For the Caledonian, McIntosh built 22 examples of his 'Dunalastair' 4-4-0s between 1910 and 1914, as well as a variety of 0-4-4Ts; Pickersgill created a number of 4-4-0 classes from 1916 to 1922; Dugald Drummond produced his 0-4-0ST 'Pugs' from 1885; and McIntosh built his 0-6-0T 'dock tanks' from 1911. The Highland had four 0-4-4Ts from 1905 specifically for the Dornoch branch, and for passenger duties Jones's 'Loch' (1896 onwards) and Peter Drummond's 'Small Ben' 4-4-0s (1898-1906) were

BALLINLUIG

Above right: Another short branch in Scotland was that to Aberfeldy from Ballinluig, on the Highland Railway route north from Perth and at the centre of the county of Perthshire. Though providing a useful service for access to Kenmore Pier, at the northern end of Loch Tay, the low demand for seats and thus the limited revenue opportunities for the branch can be seen from the provision of just one coach for No 55217 to take for the trip to Aberfeldy in August 1960. Notice, however, the neat and tidy appearance of both the station infrastructure and the trackbed, so different from so many places today. The branch and Ballinluig station – whose only real claim to fame was as the gateway to Aberfeldy, which had nearly ten times the population – closed on 3 May 1965, at the same time as all the local stations along the ex-Highland route. *Silver Link collection*

Main picture: As with many other locations featured in this book, Edinburgh (Princes Street) was a Mecca for rail enthusiasts, where express locomotives from north, south and west could be viewed alongside more local fare. One of the former is seen on 4 July 1964,

as ex-LMS 'Black 5' No 45155 leads ex-LNER 'B1' No 61245 *Murray of Elibank* out from the magnificent trainshed en route for Heads of Ayr station. The obviously excited passengers waving to their friends and relatives left behind on the platform are presumably anticipating great times at Billy Butlin's Heads of Ayr Holiday Camp. The station for this – initially built by Butlin in 1940 as a Naval Training Camp – was opened on 17 May 1947 and stayed open for this traffic until 16 September 1968. *MJS collection*

1960   EGLINTON STREET

Right: In our period, Eglinton Street was the last station on the WCML approach to Glasgow Central station and was once very busy with commuters, shoppers and other local passenger traffic, but, as with so many others, its life was cut short by changing traffic patterns and other modes of transport and it closed in 1965. Seen on 29 April 1960, both station platforms and the surrounding area are showing signs of decay, as ex-Caledonian No 55225 bustles through with empty coaching stock from a recently arrived express at Central station. *Peter Hay, Silver Link collection*

Left: Carstairs saw both express trains and more local traffic. One such is this pick-up freight, duty 'S16', behind No 57601 on 18 August 1962. The smokebox is showing signs of hard work and perhaps the engine is now more suited to this lighter task. Having served Dumfries shed for many years, its life ceased just five months after this view. *J. Schatz, Silver Link collection*

1962   CARSTAIRS

1964   EDINBURGH (Princes Street)

1962

DAWSHOLM

Left: For a period in the early 1960s, Dawsholm shed was home to a number of preserved Scottish locomotives, including ex-Caledonian Railway 4-2-2 No 123, captured on 10 July 1962 alongside 'Jones Goods' No 103. Introduced in 1886, No 123 was a design by Neilson & Co for the Caledonian and was withdrawn by the LMS (which had inherited it at the 1923 'Grouping') as No 14010 in 1935. Returned to service by BR in 1958, together with No 103, for enthusiasts' specials, this was relatively short-lived and they both now have a place in Glasgow's Transport Museum. Situated in Lanarkshire, Dawsholm shed opened for the Caledonian on 10 August 1896 and survived until 5 October 1964, after which it was demolished. *MJS*

1962

HAYMARKET

1964

GREENOCK

Right: Another example of why conditions on our steam railway failed to entice school-leavers to join! The roof of Greenock (Ladyburn) shed is obviously providing very little in the way of shelter from the wet weather on 24 August 1964, as the poor shed worker is charged with cleaning out the pit, with his barrow already well loaded. Behind, No 42216 simmers between duties, with another of the same class out in the yard. The shed was one of four to have served Greenock over the years and was built as a 10-road through shed in 1884. Second World War air raids severely damaged the structure, leaving the southernmost half uncovered until, in 1958, the remaining northlight roof was removed and those southern tracks covered by a new roof of corrugated sheeting. A partition wall to this half was constructed at the same time. Closure came on 26 November 1966, with demolition to follow. *MJS*

Main picture: A fine view of one of Gresley's finest – 'A3' No 60037 *Hyperion* – casually moving around Haymarket shed yard on a hot 13 July 1962. The driver enjoys a moment in the sun as he makes sure the photographer is safe; the 'A3' is presumably about to take charge of an express, judging by the amount of coal piled high in the tender. A thoroughbred horse that won both the Derby and St Leger in 1933, 'Hyperion' was one of the smallest horses ever to win the classic races just 15 hands 1½ inches but was also an outstanding stallion, siring winners of 752 races! The loco was equally swift in its day, operating from Edinburgh homes for most of its time, until dieselisation on the ECML and changes elsewhere saw it withdrawn in late December 1963. *MJS*

created for that company's lines. The last of the latter class, No 54398 *Ben Alder* – withdrawn in March 1953 – was scheduled for preservation but sadly, although surviving until 1966, this was not to be.

Those mentioned above, and many others, nominally in the London Midland or Eastern Regions, survived well into BR service, with a good number into the early years of the 1960s, but while the West Coast Main Line (WCML) was nowhere near the country at this stage, electrification was affecting Glasgow, and electric services such as the fabled 'Blue Train' were eating into erstwhile steam operations – despite the initial problems with transformers! Eight of Pickersgill's 4-4-0s remained on the books until 1962, with the final survivor, No 54463, not withdrawn from Polmadie shed until 22 December. No fewer than 45 of McIntosh's pre-Grouping two classes of 0-4-4Ts were in use in 1960, with Nos 55189, 55204 and 55234 summarily withdrawn on 19 January 1963, the same date as the last 'Pug', No 56029. The following week saw the end of No 56336

and McIntosh's '782' Class 0-6-0s, and numerous other 'Caley' 0-6-0 goods engines worked through the first four years of the decade. Of 'Eastern' stock, a handful of Gresley's 'K2s' were around, with the last, No 61764 *Loch Arkaig*, fighting on until 23 September 1961; all his 'K4s' went in 1961, as did the last of Reid's 'Glen' Class, No 62496 *Glen Loy*. Elsewhere, less glamorous locos went about their business, earning their keep until overtaken by events. Representatives of Reid's and Holmes's 0-6-0Ts made it through to the decade, but 1962/3 was as far as many of them went. The steam story in the country was taken over by newer designs, such as Gresley's Class 'J38' 0-6-0s – Nos 65901 and 65929 to 29 April 1967 – and interlopers like Stanier's 'Black 5s' and Thompson's 'B1s'.

1959 had seen the arrival of newly built diesels Nos D5320-46, initially to Haymarket. The following year Nos D5300-19 travelled north from Hornsey to join them; also in 1960, newly out of works, Nos D5114-32 were despatched to work from Inverness, and others were transferred north from England in

later years. It is, therefore, little wonder that the axe should have been wielded so effectively in Scotland, but there was a strange twist to the final chapter of this story. With this influx of diesels and 'Deltics' handling all southbound expresses from Edinburgh, it is perhaps surprising that, wanting to speed up the services between Glasgow and Aberdeen from

BRITISH RAILWAYS

1965

FORFAR

A sadness felt by many was seeing the disappearance of the magnificent 'A4s' from front-line work on the ECML, but happily they still managed to find suitable work in Scotland. On a bright but overcast 22 June 1965, No 60009 *Union of South Africa* speeds round the curve in Forfar station, seen from a carriage window of the 1.30pm Aberdeen-Glasgow 'Grampian Express'. Note once more how neat and tidy the railway is at this time, on and off the tracks. New in 1937, 'A4' '9' was originally numbered 4488 by the LNER, becoming No 9 during the 1946 renumbering scheme and 60009 after Nationalisation. Happily, preservation beckoned (see the next page). *Ray Ruffell, Silver Link collection*

1962, the powers that be should turn to steam! Gresley's 'A4s' – and initially a couple of 'A3s' – worked the service over the ensuing years, until the final five – Nos 60004 *William Whitelaw*, 60007 *Sir Nigel Gresley*, 60009 *Union of South Africa*, 60019 *Bittern*, 60024 *Kingfisher* and 60034 *Lord Faringdon* – finally succumbed in 1966. With now just a small freight enclave still in operation, the writing was on the wall and the steam dried up in June 1967.

On the previous day to that on page 60, No 60009 is captured from a low angle to show off the clean, sleek lines of the 'A4' as it stands at Aberdeen before beginning the run of 'The Grampian Express' on 21 June 1965. The driver and fireman peer from the depths of their cab for their portrait. A long-term servant of Haymarket shed, from where it occasionally appeared on the non-stop 'Elizabethan' run to King's Cross, it survived the cull at the close of steam on those main-line duties by transfer to Aberdeen (Ferryhill) shed on 16 June 1962. Happily, it also escaped the acetylene torch following withdrawal on 25 June 1966, being privately preserved and allowing enthusiasts in the 21st century to still enjoy the glamour and majesty of it working on both main lines and private railways. *Ray Ruffell, Silver Link collection*

1965   ABERDEEN

IT57 - THE END SUNDAY 11 AUGUST 1968
RÉQUIEM ÆTÉRNAM DONA EIS, DÓMINE; ET LUX PERPÉTUA LÚCEAT EIS.

Appropriately the funeral service for steam was to be held at the Cathedral that was, and indeed is, Liverpool's Lime Street station. This was, after all, the city from which railway passenger services had first begun in 1830 on the Liverpool & Manchester Railway.

On that black day in August 1968 it was a 'Black 5' 4-6-0, No 45110, that set forth with British Railways service IT57 - the so-called 'Fifteen Guinea Special' – that being the cost of a ticket for what we, and the 450 passengers on board, all thought would be the very last opportunity to experience real steam, out there in the wild, so to speak.

History was almost repeating itself, as the destination for this last train was to be none other than Manchester. The route, of course, would be very different, and so too would the motive power, passenger comfort levels and speeds! IT57's route and locomotive usage was as follows:

Left: And so to the end. Thankfully, through the Herculean efforts of David Porter (see the full story in your authors' *BR STEAM The Final Years 1965-68*), 'Black 5' No 45110 narrowly escaped being cut up after the end of steam on BR. It is seen on shed at Lostock Hall on 4 August 1968, alongside No 70013 *Oliver Cromwell*, in preparation for that day's special trains. *MJS*

LOSTOCK HALL

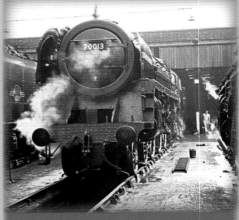

Above: Another view of Lostock Hall on 4 August 1968, as *Oliver Cromwell* is buffed up and given some TLC prior to the day's workings. *MJS*

Left: Dick Manton captured this explosive image of No 45110 bursting out of Liverpool (Lime Street) station with 'IT57' on the outward journey on 11 August 1968, officially the final day of steam working for BR. This fine loco survives and is normally based at the Severn Valley Railway. *Dick Manton*

Loco(s) used	Route
45110	Liverpool Lime Street - Rainhill - Earlestown - Eccles - Deal Street - Manchester Victoria
70013 *Oliver Cromwell*	Manchester Victoria - Windsor Bridge No.1 - Windsor Bridge No.3 - Bolton - Darwen - Blackburn - Clitheroe - Hellifield - Settle Jn - (via S&C) - Petteril Bridge Jn - Carlisle
44781 & 44871	Carlisle - (reverse of outward route) - Manchester Victoria
45110	Manchester Victoria - (reverse of outward route) - Liverpool Lime Street

1968 LIVERPOOL

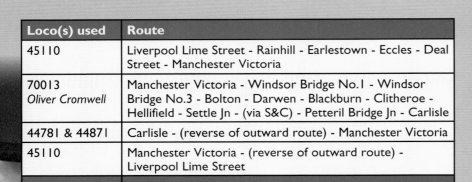

Eternal rest give to them, O Lord; and let perpetual light shine upon them...

To Dai - but not to die?

1965-1985 The Scrapyard Years

As we have seen, the rate of abandonment of steam accelerated from the mid-1950s. Elderly types were manifestly affected by the introduction of both new 'Standard' steam locos and the emergence of ever greater numbers of diesels and electrics (locos and EMUs), but in addition to changing traffic patterns the gradual downgrading of more modern types to handle less prestigious duties also played its part.

1963   **DARLINGTON**

Above: With the increasing number of locomotives being withdrawn from 1960 onwards, BR's own workshops found it increasingly difficult to cope with the scrapping demands, as seen here at Darlington Works on 7 March 1964. Wrested from their frames, the boilers of Nos 68042, 42150 and 68024 have had some initial cutting attention, but their smokebox numbers remain intact! *MJS*

Right: As time passed, the sheer speed of withdrawals overwhelmed BR's works sites and saw locos stored and abandoned in all manner of temporary places, such as alongside the main line at Chesterfield, where 'B1'

1966   **CHESTERFIELD**

No 61361 stands with others and wagons in Garnham, Harris & Elton's Lockerford Sidings on 6 March 1966. *MJS*

STRATFORD

An additional problem was where to temporarily store BR's officially preserved locomotives until an appropriate place could be found for them. Several of the engines concerned were transported to various locations, including two in Leicester, with old steam sheds being a favourite. Stratford shed, on the eastern fringes of London, saw a healthy collection at one point, stored in an abandoned building. On 7 May 1967 an enthusiast enjoys the possibility of cabbing No 70000 *Britannia* and viewing the line of others in front. Among those also 'on shed' that day were Nos 30925 *Cheltenham*, 30850 *Lord Nelson* and 49395. *MJS*

At the close of 1959 there were around 14,500 steam locos still 'on the books', although many of these were not active, being either in works, out of steam, on shed awaiting attention, or unofficially cast aside, many with ragged chimneys denoting their status. By and large, BR's own works had thus far dealt with the relevant scrapping needs, but the increasing rapidity of withdrawals was leading to thousands of engines scattered at all points of the compass around the UK. Swindon and Darlington were just two that constantly had partly dismantled 'dead bodies' lying around their sites with ever more potentially knocking at the door. Something had to be done.

The eventual explosion in private yards taking the overspill was not immediate, but fairly quickly many contractors saw the earnings potential and weighed in, some to a much greater extent than others. George Cohen's and John Cashmore's companies handled hundreds – and thousands in

1967 NORTH BLYTH

Main picture: More evidence of the rapidity of the influx of diesels: a line of abandoned steam at the side of North Blyth shed on an incredibly (and appropriately) dull 1 July 1967 is being studied by members of Thurmaston Railway Society. Heading the line are Nos 43071 and 62062, respectively withdrawn from North Blyth on 22 April 1967 (and scrapped at Arnott Young, in Dinsdale, the following November) and 15 July 1967. Opened in 1894 by the North Eastern Railway, and with a ramped coaling stage, the gable-roofed roundhouse at North Blyth – off to the right – closed just two months after this visit. *MJS*

the latter case – while other yards saw only a small handful, in some cases just one loco! Details of precisely what was cut where has been open to misinterpretation and/or error over the years. The need for accurate disposal details of BR's steam locomotive fleet has been recognised by a group of committed and determined enthusiasts, who have access to official company records and who have set up a website – www.whatreallyhappenedtosteam.co.uk. This is to provide a contact point and home for records from those individuals who made personal observations or visits to sites. Published books from the accumulated data are to follow.

In view of the uncertainty and inaccuracies of much information on this aspect of our railway's history – and as the published findings of the website's authors were not published at the time of writing – your authors have chosen to publish some of the records from their own scrapyard visits. Notes of locos merely in store at depots have been ignored; only instances where cutting was involved have been included. We hope that you will understand the reasoning behind this and that the information now given, however limited, will be of interest.

1965 NEW ENGLAND

Right: A remarkable survivor! 'K3' No 61912 is seen on New England (Peterborough) shed on 7 March 1965 and looks to be ready for work, with coal piled high on the tender, but the coupling and connecting rods are missing! A Lincolnshire resident for many years, it finally moved to King's Cross 'Top Shed' on 21 April 1962, but for just six months before disposal on 6 October; in truth, it should then have made a trip to the scrap man, but stay of execution came with its use as a stationary boiler at New England. When seen here, it had just lost this battle and the final curtain was about to fall, at Cashmore's yard, Great Bridge, in May 1965. *MJS*

1967

SUNDERLAND

The date is 1 July 1967 and Thurmaston Railway Society has moved on from North Blyth to Sunderland, but the weather has not improved! Two club members casually stroll along the line of yet more stored locos, collecting the numbers, with No 63436 at the head of the line. The North East was one of the last regions to dispense with steam, but by this date the process was accelerating. Withdrawn on 27 May 1967 from Sunderland, this NER Raven-designed 'Q6' had spent much of its working life to October 1963 in the York/Hull area, handling the many mineral trains to and from the Docks. Sunderland South Dock engine shed was graced with both a roundhouse and a straight shed, and closed to steam on 17 September 1967, after which the roundhouse was demolished. The straight shed then survived as a diesel depot until the 1980s, when it too was razed to the ground. *MJS*

SWINDON WORKS

20 September 1959

6716; 9491; 5160; 4217; 9438; 6359; 4221; 7705; 1457; 9417; 9427; 7416; 5734; 7415; 6734; 9403; 6397; 9492; 8434; 5784; 6730?; 5721; 5010; 2838; 4560; 1428; 5424; 6743;

2 September 1962

8764; 3404; 7799; 7764; 7323; 8100; 4086; 6023; 4274; 4235; 5024; 5035; 5996; 5012; 6376; 4974; 2255; 2853; 6157; 6101; 6348; 7334; 6120; 6302; 1435; 5187; 5758; 9703; 6013; 6336; 5180; 4986; 4293; 6778; 5906; 5941; 7720; 5947;

28 April 1963

8791; 3769; 9412; 8472; 8738; 5775; 8703; 1023; 5956; 6119; 8710; 9727; 6348; 7334; 8770; 6422; 9759; 9747; 8773; 9775; 5931; 7314; 6101; 6369; 5023; 8776; 9652; 8737; 6962; 9725; 5912; 3736; 1435;

20 October 1963

*9633; 3652; 3653; 4690; 9763; 3769; 3766; 8738; 9412; 3668; 9700; 6025; 6026; 6011; 6835; 5995; 3711; 9793; 8458; 6666; 9479; 9440; 1621; 8791; 5201; 9401; 9764; 8491; 4629; 6674; 5787; 5645; 6631; 6609; 4134; 6632; 9636; 1608; 4651; 1471; 6416; 6138; 6919; 4682;

22 March 1964

1020; 4706; 2818; 8738; 9752; 9603; 1666; 1650; 9425; 5683; 3733; 4644; 5573; 3668; 6010; 3665; 5623; 6682; 9420; 5787; 47557; 9429; 7251; 1614; 5685; 4275; 6120; 7430; 3841;

10 May 1964

9484; 9489; 2818; 1666; 9425; 8738; 9752; 9431; 1447; 8102; 3721; 9743; 1650; 8494; 3665; 6680; 5683; 6682; 47623; 6010; 9420; 5057; 9603; 4706; 6824; 6603; 5787; 8732; 6771; 4652; 7738; 8456; 5947;

11 October 1964

4659; 9425; 9457; 8405; 8409; 60889; 60809; 6010; 6824; 9484; 6873; 8418; 2818; 60916; 60942; 60812; 60809; 78009; 60922; 3748; 60945; 8401; 60941; 60887; 6000; 60932; 60856; 5264; 4626; 5602; 9752; 6825;

CREWE WORKS

27 July 1960

40653; 40655;

30 September 1962

42678; 52441; 52312; 49025; 49002; 49147; 49139; 49034; 52093; 51412; 48953; 49125; 49126; 45513; 45551; 45548; 45524; 49301;

NEW ENGLAND 1965

December 1947, were at Norwich, Leicester Central, Colwick, Annesley, Lincoln and, for five months, King's Cross, before arrival at New England in April 1959. It was sold for scrap in January 1966 to Garnham, Harris & Elton's at Lockerford, Chesterfield. *MJS*

Below left: A throw-back to a previous age, old rodded ground signals are pictured at Wroxham on 5 October 1991. *Ray Ruffell, Silver Link collection*

Bottom right: There were times when it was difficult to note from external conditions whether a locomotive had been placed into store, but there is no doubt here! On 1 July 1967, with the sun now out, compared to the views at North Blyth and Sunderland, No 63397 stands forlorn at West Hartlepool shed, with several parts of the loco plainly out of use, though not officially withdrawn until a fortnight later, after many years of service solely from this depot. *MJS*

Above: Not exactly out with the old and in with the new, but while No 61912 was no longer in use at New England as a stationary boiler on 7 March 1965, 'B1' No 61272 – numbered 'Departmental Locomotive No 25' from January to November 1965 –was still in steam on the same day and in the same role. In this case, however, the engine had been a New England incumbent when withdrawn on 9 January 1965, and had presumably therefore taken over from the 'K3'. Its previous homes, after appearing new in

DERBY WORKS

27 August 1960
42390; 43840; 42399; 42346; 44103; 47563; 47303; 44052; 42326; 44031; 47205; 47652; 44423; 44585; 43484; 40047; 43394; 47203; 40489; 43218; 58116; 47560; 44406; 40652; 43866; 44515; 41773; 58126; 47265; 40633; 43946; 44029; 47274; 47561;

2 July 1961
44175?; 42332; 44148; 43787; 41173; 41532; 42510; 42531; 42502; 42501; 58246; 43846; 43905; 42307; 42506; 42344; 44067; 47268; 4238047268; 40124; 43868; 43771; 41103;

1967 WEST HARTLEPOOL

Derby (cont.)   25 August 1962
41150; 44122; 47463; 47420;
43985; 44020; 47259; 43826;
42367; 42348; 42356; 44158;
42500; 42305; 58246; 42342;
47268; 47678; 44067; 42531;
47473; 44122; 42420; 40537;
42385; 47457; 47403; 41529;
47310; 47275; 47508; 47483;
47422; 47601; 42375; 42393;
41536; 42387; 43216; 42352;
47545; 43682; 47426; 47630;

Though steam on parts of the Southern Region was still in operation in 1966, there were still casualties that found themselves stored at depots, like No 82018 at Nine Elms in 1966, still a relatively young loco. New on 7 October 1952 to Exmouth Junction shed, it moved eastwards to Eastleigh after ten years, then to London two months later. Withdrawn on 22 August 1966, it was then despatched to South Wales to be cut at J. Buttigieg's yard, Newport, within a month. *MJS*

1966   NINE ELMS SHED

1965   BUXTON

Below: Even named locos were not exempt from the ongoing cull, as exemplified by chimney-less 'Patriot' No 45522 *Prestatyn* at Buxton on 28 March 1965. Also devoid of name, smokebox number and shedplate, it stands abandoned in a siding at the edge of the shed, together with an ex-LMS 4F 0-6-0, also without chimney. Was the shed short of plant-pots? *Prestatyn* was first-class WCML motive power at Camden until a move to the Midland lines in November 1959, but this was relatively short-lived, as a move to Manchester came in September 1961, to Newton Heath, then Longsight. The short trip to Buxton for storage came after withdrawal on 3 October 1964. *MJS*

KETTERING

Above: With the overflows at BR works, private scrapyards increasingly took up the slack. George Cohen's yard at Kettering began taking many locos from the southern half of the UK, including ex-GWR and ex-SR types. On a sunny 24 May 1964 No 5018 *St Mawes Castle* has pride of place, with an ex-SR 'Schools' and 'S15' behind. A rake of London Underground stock stands to the right. New from Swindon Works in 1932, this was a sad fate to befall such a glamorous engine as the 'Castle' after only 32 years in service. A well-travelled loco, it had been utilised by Bristol, Swindon, Worcester, Gloucester, Hereford and, finally, Reading, leaving there in April 1964 to travel north to Kettering. *MJS*

Below: The 'S15' at the far end of the row above is seen again on the same day. No 30507 still has its smokebox number and, despite losing its coupling rods, is basically intact, complete with eight-wheeled tender. A Feltham engine for most of its life, its demise came on 6 January 1964, so it took slightly longer to reach the Midlands than the 'Castle', but was quicker than the 'Schools'. Final despatch was not immediate but was completed within months. *MJS*

DONCASTER WORKS

17 September 1961
69549; 61920; 61891; 69580; 69543;

28 October 1962
42219; 90087; 61825; 42687; 42502; 65567; 60943; 42527; 61091; 68914; 68911

DARLINGTON WORKS

17 September 1961
67707; 61432; 67760; 68316; 68702; 67665; 61466; 67769; 68687; 67717; 67740; 68737; 68693; 61445; 68745; 67670; 65779; 68145; 68708; 68686; 69921; 65778; 61456; 62739; 62716; 62734; 68033; 68078;

HORWICH WORKS

21 April 1963

– 21/4/63
44508; 44388; 40083; 52515;
47402; 42724; 44019; 42655;
42935; 42862; 44474; 42270;
42939; 44579; 44407; 44152;
42893; 42929; 42887; 44573;
42775; 42891; 44553; 51207;
40073; 40120

KETTERING (COHEN'S)

24 May 1964

5018; 30917; 33024; 30507; 30153;
30901; 30920; 30935;

25 February 1967

48225; 47521; 47658; 47649;
46519; 43018; 48514; 48527; 3605;
92013; 48755; 47318; 47396;

15 April 1967

43018; 48514; 48527; 3605; 48088;
48372; 48270; 92013; 48755;
47318; 47396; 47435;

1967

KETTERING

Left: With the help of some unknown
kind individual, we have clear
identification and confirmation of
the cabside number of No 45240
at Kettering on 30 July 1967.
Taken from the empty tender of
another locomotive, the 'Black 5'
is just one of the line of engines
awaiting the cutter's attention;
debris from previous victims can
be seen alongside the row to the
right. The site was in the wilds of
Northamptonshire, on an old branch
striking west from Kettering station
and approached from a narrow
country road, the bridge for which
can be seen in the distance. It is plain
that the site had restricted available
space and the company did well to
despatch so many so efficiently. No
45240 had been withdrawn from
Stoke shed just six months earlier,
having spent much of its life working
from the two Crewe sheds. *MJS*

16 February 1963

67648; 61267; 65871; 67610;
65797; 65877; 67639; 65033;
68055; 60927; 65099; 61339;
60842; 60927; 60879; 61296;
61297; 67679; 60807; 64915;
67716; 69921; 64821; 64730;
67673; 67685; 65695; 67617;
67631; 67622; 61419; 67761;
61415; 69017; 64939; 69026;
65769; 64835; 64758; 61443;
60801; 60878; 67603; 67744;
67784; 67748; 67665; 69101;
67712; 67782;

7 March 1964

68061; 42407; 68024; 41250;
67744; 68042; 67632; 67623;
67680; 63390; 68180; 68149;
68039; 47589; 90624; 60924;
43987; 63424; 90607; 63460;
60802; 65033; 65099;

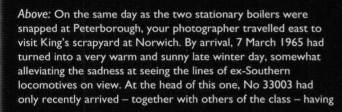

1965

NORWICH

Above: On the same day as the two stationary boilers were snapped at Peterborough, your photographer travelled east to visit King's scrapyard at Norwich. By arrival, 7 March 1965 had turned into a very warm and sunny late winter day, somewhat alleviating the sadness at seeing the lines of ex-Southern locomotives on view. At the head of this one, No 33003 had only recently arrived – together with others of the class – having

been sold to the company that January. Withdrawn from Feltham shed on 22 June 1964, it was new from Brighton Works in May 1942, ready for the war effort, and its unusual Bulleid design was greeted by a mixture of horror and uncertainty. Its original number under its designer's designation was 'C3' and it carried this into Nationalisation in 1948, not being renumbered by BR until relatively late, in January 1951. Its first allocation was Guildford, until a move to Tonbridge in 1959.

30 July 1967
45276; 76036; 48270; 45240; 48739; 42224; 42083;

28 October 1967
76008; 44853; 44696; 44870; 76095; 76041; 44860; 45003; 45024; 42267; 44930; 92090; 45019; 45070; 42086; 42133; 45147; 48721; 48394; 43130; 44695; 48542; 48256; 43129; 45303

7 April 1969
48467; 44816;

COWLAIRS WORKS
25 August 1964
55189; 42876; 64963; 64929; 61305; 65913;

NEWPORT (CASHMORE'S)
4 September 1964
7307; 4964; 5980; 6330; 5038; 3858; 5937; 4934; 1001; 5247; 5097; 7247; 5253; 5994; 5231; 5537; 4574; 3679; 5555; 5548; 5568; 31623; 3629; 6438; 4570; 4567; 4642; 6320

Yard 1 - 19 April 1966
6111; 4113; 82041; 4161; 9680; 42247; 7829; 6856; 6141; 92230; 9672; 34076;

Yard 2 - 19 April 1966
84000; 92244; 92250; 45188; 44835; 34052; 34036

17 March 1968
45373; 45107; 73071; 73043; 73118; 34087;

Above: Elsewhere on site that day, surrounded by the remains of previous unlucky visitors, was No 30546, which first saw the light of day on 23 June 1939, Nine Elms being its first home. It was fitted with a new chimney in September 1946 and renumbered by BR on 27 January 1950. Most of its time was spent working from Horsham and Three Bridges, before a trip west to Bournemouth on 6 January 1964, for just six months. It, too, was sold to King's in January 1965. *Both MJS*

1967   **KETTERING**

Above right: Another view of Kettering on 30 July 1967 shows No 48270 perilously close to its end with, again, signs of previous unfortunates scattered around. Kirkby-in-Ashfield had been

its long-term home, before a move to Derby in 1959, then a whirlwind tour of depots – three changes within 12 months – up to the end on 31 December 1966. *MJS*

NEWPORT (BUTTIGIEG)		
19 April 1966		
42103; 84002; 82022; 34033; 31858;		

NEWPORT (UNITED WAGON)		
19 April 1966		
34008; 34047; 34104; 34108; 34098; 82031; 82034; 82003; 48249; 73002; 73016; 46484; 92127; 34017; 92050; 48618		

NORWICH (KING'S)		
7 March 1965		
33033; 30546; 33006; 33003; 33030; 31827; 31400;		

GREAT BRIDGE (Cashmore's)		
25 July 1965		
90225; 90136; 90202; 92038; 90188; 63717; 63902; 43037; 90115; 63793; 43067; 6906; 90383; 90085; 42556; 5056; 90346;		

Another sign of the hurried times, when scrapyards attacked the incumbents with gusto just to keep on top of the near avalanche of incoming locomotives. The haste in cutting is exemplified by the summary removal of the smokebox of No 90383, still complete with its smokebox numberplate, at Cashmore's yard in Great Bridge, Birmingham, on 25 July 1965. *MJS*

BARRY DOCKS

To many in the railway fraternity, the name of Dai Woodham is spoken in awe and reverence and for equal numbers he deserved to be knighted 'for services to railway preservation'! His part in our story started quietly enough, as he mopped up hundreds of locomotives and wagons discarded as surplus by BR. That subsequent societies and individuals were able to rescue over 200 engines from his Barry Docks scrapyard is more by good fortune than any avowed intention on his part, arising from his ability to turn over cash more quickly for much of the time by scrapping the wagons while the locos 'rotted' in the sea air around him. But we who now enjoy seeing those resurrected also owe a debt to his humanity and tolerance, as thousands of spotters and more general enthusiasts descended on his site over a number of years, giving access and stimulation to those who were to save their pet monster.

A fuller story is available elsewhere, but here are few salient facts:
- The first locos arrived on 25 March 1959 – Nos 5312, 5360, 5392 and 5397 – from Swindon Works
- In total nine arrived that year and all were cut, including No 3170, the last Class '3150' 2-6-2T
- 19 arrived in 1960 and only one – No 4164 – was cut
- 1962 saw the first 'Kings' arrive – Nos 6023 *King Edward II* and 6024 *King Edward I*
- 1964 saw the greatest influx – 74 in total, including five 'Castles', nine Bulleid 'Pacifics' and one 'Jubilee'
- 1968 saw the first departure – No 43924 – to the Keighley & Worth Valley Railway
- 1969 was the first year for a decade with no incomers, but Nos 5322 and 31618 departed
- 1973-5 saw the most leave each year – 18, 19 and 14 – until another peak, at 21, in 1981

1965   **GREAT BRIDGE**

While both of your authors made a number of visits to Barry, only John had the foresight to make copious separate notes. Following are records he made – in the order that locos were seen - from just two random dates:

Above: A second view of parts of No 90383 at Great Bridge on the same day, this time one set of driving wheels from the 'Austerity' 2-8-0, never to travel on rails again!

Below: Elsewhere on site that day – but with the sun now having become shy! – two variants of Robinson's 'O4' 2-8-0s line up. No 63717 was one of the type introduced in 1917 for the Royal Ordnance Department during the First World War, having steam brakes and no water scoop in the tender, whereas No 63902 was of the number introduced in 1924, rebuilt from Class 'O5', with a higher cab and no side windows. Both were Langwith Junction residents for around two decades and both were removed from active stock on the same day, 17 April 1965, with transfer to Birmingham shortly afterwards. *Both MJS*

29 June 1963
5182, 5547, 9445, 9449, 9499, 7723, 5422, 9491, 8419, 5510, 9462, 5558, 7722, 9468, 5794, 5557, 5552, 5553, 5542, 5538, 5572, 5539, 4566, 5521, 4561, 5193, 4588, 5532, 5526, 6023, 6024, 5541, 4270, 4253.

Subsequently cut were:
5182 (1964), 5510, 5547, 5557, 5558, 7722, 7723, 8419, 9445, 9449, 9462, 9468, 9491, and 9499 (1965)

20 June 1965
92207, 34072, 34092, 3845, 35006, 34028, 34016, 7903, 5952, 35009, 35025, 30830, 35018, 34027, 3612, 9629, 34070, 5541, 4270, 6024, 5227, 4213, 4278, 6023, 7220, 5526, 34105, 5532, 30541, 4588, 5193,

92245, 4561, 5521, 2873, 4566, 2859, 5539, 5572, 3814, 5542, 34081, 5553, 34067, 5552, 5557, 34073, 5794, 9468, 34058, 7722, 5558, 45699, 3794, 4942, 4979, 7027, 5029, 5972, 5043, 31806, 31638, 31625, 30825, 4277, 31618, 6695, 53808, 5619, 3822, 5967, 7202, 4936, 2885, 6960, 6619, 6989, 6692, 53809, 7200, 48431, 5224, 4953, 30506, 5080, 5164, 30847, 2874, 5199, 30828, 5239, 30499, 2857, 30841, 4141, 4248, 5051, 2861, 2807, 3803, 45690, 4983, 5900, 4930, 31874, 5637, 7325, 6634, 5322, 4247, 6636, 5668, 9466,

Subsequently cut were:
3794, 5557, 5558, 5794, 7722 and 9468 (1965)

1965   **GREAT BRIDGE**

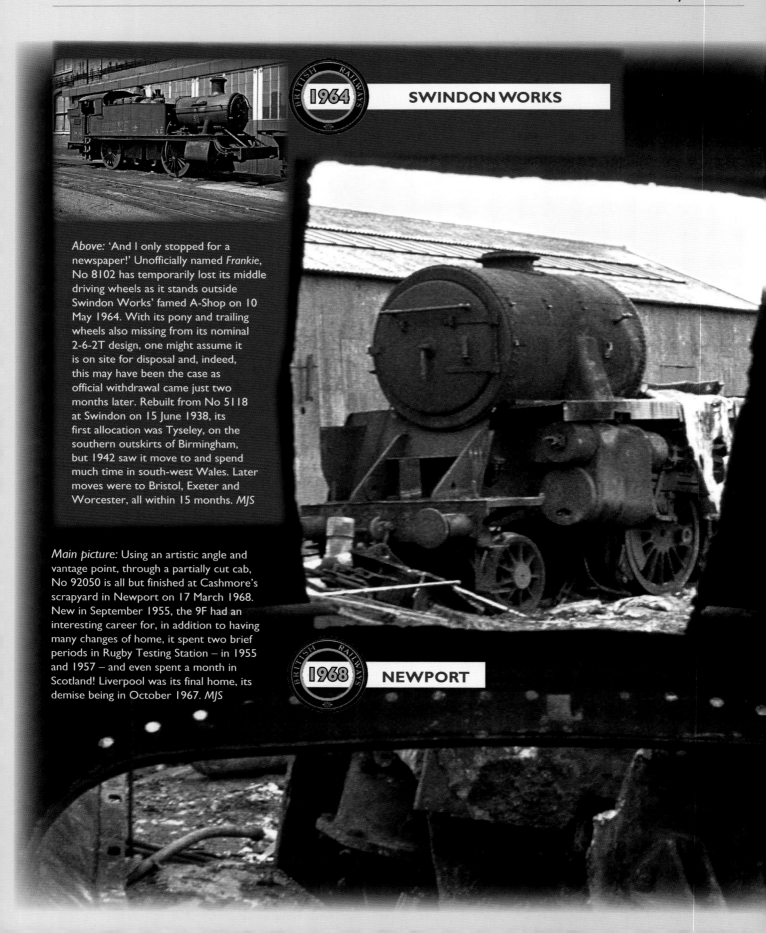

1964

SWINDON WORKS

Above: 'And I only stopped for a newspaper!' Unofficially named *Frankie*, No 8102 has temporarily lost its middle driving wheels as it stands outside Swindon Works' famed A-Shop on 10 May 1964. With its pony and trailing wheels also missing from its nominal 2-6-2T design, one might assume it is on site for disposal and, indeed, this may have been the case as official withdrawal came just two months later. Rebuilt from No 5118 at Swindon on 15 June 1938, its first allocation was Tyseley, on the southern outskirts of Birmingham, but 1942 saw it move to and spend much time in south-west Wales. Later moves were to Bristol, Exeter and Worcester, all within 15 months. *MJS*

Main picture: Using an artistic angle and vantage point, through a partially cut cab, No 92050 is all but finished at Cashmore's scrapyard in Newport on 17 March 1968. New in September 1955, the 9F had an interesting career for, in addition to having many changes of home, it spent two brief periods in Rugby Testing Station – in 1955 and 1957 – and even spent a month in Scotland! Liverpool was its final home, its demise being in October 1967. *MJS*

1968

NEWPORT

1962   SWINDON WORKS

Right: Whether visited on the ground or seen from a passing train, Swindon Works was a goldmine for spotters, with lines of engines, either fresh out of or waiting to go into the Works complex, together with those awaiting their fate at the hands of the scrapmen. Here a string of the latter is seen from a train in 1962, with one of the once mighty 'Kings' nearest the camera. No 6006 *King George I* was first to go, from Wolverhampton (Stafford Road) shed in February 1962 when exactly 34 years old, and the whole class was extinct within 12 months. It had run 1,593,367 miles by the end, the fourth lowest mileage of the 30. *Ray Ruffell, Silver Link collection*

1968   NEWPORT

Below: A wider view of part of Cashmore's famous yard in Newport, with No 45188 lined up to be the next for the chop on 17 March 1968, surrounded by wheels, chimneys and various other 'innards' of items already dealt with and the crane ready for its next task. The 'Black 5' was another well-travelled locomotive, and records would seem to indicate that a fair part of its total mileage was moving between depots! Spending virtually the whole of its working life on the WCML, it finally succumbed to the inevitable at Speke Junction shed on 9 September 1967, with the move to South Wales not too long thereafter. *MJS*

DAI WOODHAM'S YARD

1968

BARRY

To most railway enthusiasts, Dai Woodham was a saint, for without him we would not have the many locomotives that now grace our preserved railways. Had it not been for his decision to amass a stock of engines, but to make smaller money more often by scrapping wagons at a crucial part of our history, the engines on this and the next three pages would have disappeared to make so many catfood tins!

Above: Somewhat imitating Joseph and his coat of many colours, with the rust vying to overtake and outdo the previous livery, No 5322 awaits its (at the time) uncertain fate at Barry Docks on 17 March 1968. Arriving at Barry in 1965, after withdrawal from Pontypool Road, it was privately purchased in 1969 and initially moved to Caerphilly, where it was returned to steam in 1971. A subsequent move took it to Didcot, where it stayed. *MJS*

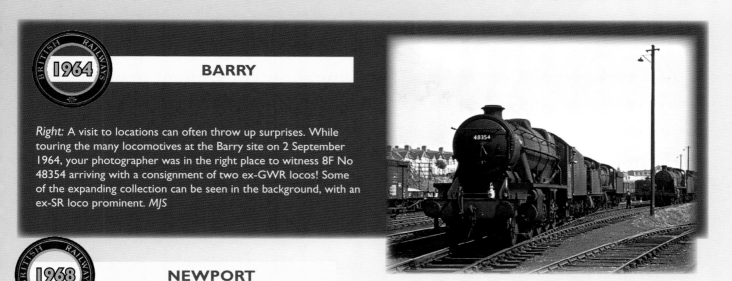

1964

BARRY

Right: A visit to locations can often throw up surprises. While touring the many locomotives at the Barry site on 2 September 1964, your photographer was in the right place to witness 8F No 48354 arriving with a consignment of two ex-GWR locos! Some of the expanding collection can be seen in the background, with an ex-SR loco prominent. *MJS*

1968

NEWPORT

Main picture: Over the years there have been countless pictures of the rows of more than 200 locomotives stored at Dai Woodham's site, and many thousands visited to either pay homage to past glories, investigate whether such-and-such loco was worth saving, or just to

look. There were, however, other scrapyards in close proximity, and on 17 March 1968 No 34108 *Wincanton* looks in remarkably good condition as it awaits its fate, in company with sister loco No 34104 *Bere Alston,* at United Wagon, Newport. New in April 1950, in Bulleid's 'air-smoothed' shape, No 34108 was originally named *Blandford,* until October 1952; rebuilding to the form seen here came at Eastleigh in May 1961. *MJS*

20 April 1966 was another gloriously sunny day at Barry and we are here 'in among 'em'! To the left, closest to the camera, is No 5972 *Olton Hall*, with Nos 5029 *Nunney Castle* and 7027 *Thornbury Castle* in front, while to the right No 30828 towers above on the embankment. *MJS*

BRITISH RAILWAYS

1966

BARRY

Inset below: On the same day your photographer's car is 'to the Manor born', standing alongside four ex-GWR 'Manor' 4-6-0s. From right to left, No 7822 *Foxcote Manor* heads the row, followed by 7819 *Hinton Manor*, 7821 *Ditcheat Manor* and 7817 *Garsington Manor*, all seemingly in fair condition, although missing their nameplates and cabside numberplates. *MJS*

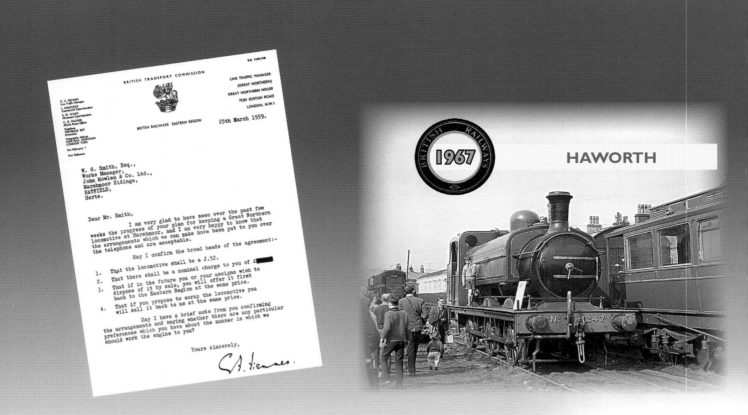

Above: Letter of sale from BR to the late Capt Bill Smith. *Silver Link collection*

Above right: Out of steam at Haworth in 1967. *Ray Ruffell, Silver Link collection*

Below: A brief moment of rest at Grosmont on the NYMR, on 20 June 1976, before setting off on the climb to Goathland and on to Pickering. *MJS*

Main picture: At Hatfield on 14 April 1962, at the head of the SLS (Midland Area) 'Tour of Seven Branch Lines' rail tour, which also included Nos 40026 and 40646 and had begun at Birmingham (New Street). No 1247 was entrusted with the stretch from Hitchin to Luton GN, via Hertford North, Welwyn Garden City and Hatfield. Notice the near-appropriate headcode of '1X47'!

GROSMONT

THE RISE OF STEAM

THE PRESERVATION PIONEERS 1959 - 1968

Since the very early days certain locomotives had been selected for preservation, initially by the individual railways, so No 1247 is not even close to being the first. However, it was the first standard gauge locomotive sold from British Railways service to a private individual, and is therefore an important element in our story. Designed by Henry Ivatt, it was built in May 1899 by Sharp Stewart & Co for the Great Northern Railway and inherited by the LNER in 1923, which classified the 0-6-0ST and its sisters as Class 'J52'. Renumbered 68846 by BR, it was withdrawn from King's Cross 'Top Shed' on 23 May 1959, preserved by Capt Bill Smith and more latterly presented to the National Railway Museum in York. At the time of writing, it is resident in the Locomotion Museum at Shildon. We have here three views of it in service.

1247 AND EARLY PRESERVED LOCOMOTIVES

1962

HATFIELD

1967

TOTNES

Below left: As with the mass scrapping days of the early/mid-1960s, the sudden realisation that valuable artefacts of a past glory could soon disappear brought preservationists out in force, but in those early times there was not the plethora of available sites to accommodate the

salvaged materials, and locos began popping up in strange places. On such was near the cattle market in Totnes, where Churchward's Cl '1361' 1910-vintage No 1363 was seen on 22 August 1967.

Below right: Just behind, on the same day, was No 6998 *Burton Agnes Hall*. Built in 1949, it was still a relatively young loco, although built to a GWR design. Disposal had come on 15 January 1966 at Oxford but the nascent Great Western Society determined that it and No 1363 should not perish. Ultimately both were transferred from this temporary incarceration at Totnes to find their way to Didcot. *Both MJS*

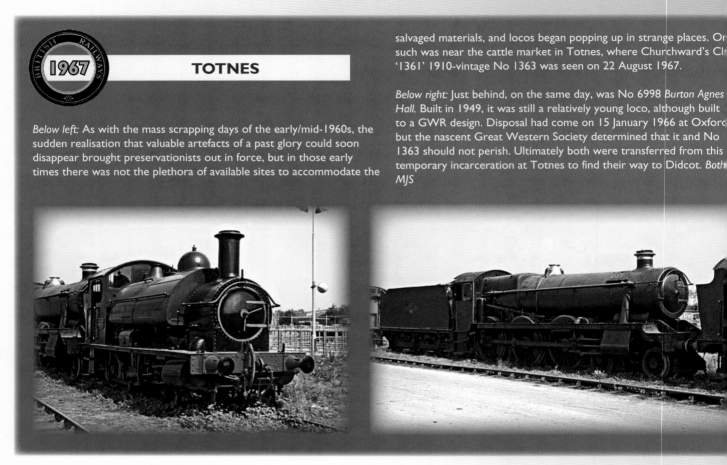

Below: Over the years the National Railway Museum in York acquired many locomotives for the National Collection, to be displayed inside what was York engine shed. Space quickly became a problem, leading to the decision to allow certain of their number to have outings on the growing number of preserved lines. On 27

March 1982 'Improved Director' No 506 *Butler-Henderson* slowly moves from the shed, in the left background, towards Loughborough Central station. Decked out in pseudo-GCR livery and original number, it is not out of place, as towards the end of its life it ran through this station as BR No 62660 on evening Nottingham Victoria-Leicester Central local trains. New from Gorton Works in 1919, it was named after one of the GCR Directors and is now the sole remaining GCR passenger locomotive. *MJS collection*

1982

LOUGHBOROUGH

BUCKFASTLEIGH

Centre right: Another view of No 1369, but this time in full pseudo-GWR regalia at Ashburton in August 1970.

Below: No 6435, with coaches and headlamp, looks ready to go! One of three Class '6400' locos preserved, it was built in 1937 at Swindon and spent most of its life in South Wales. Its final home was St Blazey, in Cornwall, until 12 October 1964. Since preservation, mostly on the Paignton & Dartmouth Steam Railway, it has also travelled widely. *All MJS*

What was to become the South Devon Railway Trust began life as the Dart Valley Railway, when in 1969 the station site at Buckfastleigh and the line north to Ashburton was occupied. The railway has had a sometimes turbulent existence since, not least in losing that northern stretch to the building of the A38 'Expressway' across the route. At the time of these views, 22 August 1967, none of the locos were actually in steam, but it is pleasing to report that all have made progress over the years and many have seen service at a variety of heritage sites.

Top left: No 1450, built in 1935 and originally numbered 4850, is currently preserved on the Dean Forest Railway.

Top right: No 1369 is seen here in a form of undercoat. Built to a Collett design at Swindon in 1934, it spent many years negotiating the tight clearances on the line to Weymouth Quay, handling boat trains. It moved to Totnes in 1965 after withdrawal from Wadebridge shed the previous October.

Centre left: No 1466 has received some early external paintwork. New in 1936, it lost the battle for life in December 1963 at Taunton shed. It is now based at Didcot.

HAWORTH

1968   1976

Left: 'Black 5' No 45212 stands at Haworth on 16 November 1968, just three months after its survival to the end of steam on BR and a month after the move to the K&WVR. Built by Armstrong Whitworth for the LMS in November 1935, it spent most of its life in the North West and had the honour of being the last BR steam loco to shunt at Preston.

Centre left: Devoid of boiler cladding, No 52044, here masquerading as L&YR No 957 (its original number), was new in 1887 from Beyer Peacock. At withdrawal it had logged up 1,154,163 miles, with most of its time having been spent in the North East, especially Wakefield and Goole.

Above: By 26 June 1976 No 52044 has resumed its BR identity and has also had a new coat of BR unlined black. Waiting for an emblem on the tender, it is otherwise apparently ready for work.

Left: Originally introduced as No 13000, from Horwich Works in 1926, this loco was allocated the number 2700 when the new Ivatt Class 4 2-6-0 locos – allotted numbers beginning 3000 – emerged in 1947. Preserved by the NRM after withdrawal in March 1966, it is one of the very few of the early locos to gain sanctuary that has not been restored for touring around the heritage lines and/or on the main line. *All MJS*

Right: Work has begun on ex-MR No 3924 at Haworth on 16 November 1968, with firebox and dome both in receipt of fresh paint. Built in 1920 at Derby Works, it spent many years working from Gloucester (Barnwood) but finished up, for the last three years, at Bristol (Barrow Road). Withdrawal was on 11 July 1965.

Below: What a mess! Seen at Haworth on 16 November 1968, Ex-LMS No 11243 looks more ready for scrap than restoration, but thankfully the boys at the K&WVR were nothing if not determined...!

Bottom: right ...and what a difference a few years can make! Seen on 26 June 1976, the transformation is almost unbelievable. One of a class introduced in 1910, this is what it must have looked like when first out of the works, as L&YR No 19.

Bottom: Finally, another loco that had received attention towards its return to operating status when seen at Haworth on 26 June 1976. One of the few built at Swindon, to help the LMS satisfy wartime demands, it appeared in March 1944 but did not enter LMS stock until three years later. Its BR number was applied in November 1949 and it arrived at the K&WVR in May 1972, having spent nearly eight years at Barry Docks. *All MJS*

Left: Following the establishment of a presence at Tyseley, the next step was to invite and encourage visitors. Two working former main-line locos helped, and ex-LMS No 45593 *Kolhapur* is seen giving rides on a line leading to the BR tracks on 13 September 1970. Note the 'period' flared trousers worn by the couple close to the loco.

Below: The other present was from the GWR stable. No 7029 *Clun Castle* is at the other end of the train on this day in 1970, and the fact that both were 'nose-first' from the train was a boon for photographers.

Bottom: Moving forward two years, the weather was most certainly less kind in October 1972. In between heavy rain showers No 30777 *Sir Lamiel* is without nameplates and front number but is adorned with the second of the two BR logos on the tender. *All MJS*

1970 TYSELEY 1972

Viewed in 2010, the proliferation and availability of preserved steam locos is a given, and, it is fairly safe to say, taken for granted by many. Many of the so-called lost causes have been resurrected and with the increasing number of 'new builds' it is easy to slip into being blasé regarding the feast currently on offer – but it was not always thus. In 1959, when No 1247 was saved, there were still most of the 'glamorous' locomotives still in active service; the idea of trying to save either a line or a loco was still in its infancy and regarded by many as lunacy and/or folly. Only 15 years from the end of the Second World War, the country was still climbing out of the aftermath of the conflict and money was by no means plentiful; it was not fashionable to become involved with railways and few men of means (and it was usually men!) had any inclination to do such a thing. Alan Pegler was looked on with derision in some parts for his financial involvement with the rescue of the Ffestiniog Railway – but there were straws in the wind.

What became the Didcot Railway Centre (overleaf) began life as the Great Western Society. Aware of events that presaged the eventual eradication of their beloved ex-GWR locomotives, a hardy group of individuals successfully acquired a handful of representative engines over time and these were initially spread among three main sites – Totnes (see page 82), Ashchurch and Taplow. Nos 6106, 6998 Burton Agnes Hall and 1466 formed a nucleus of what became a growing group, and eventually a unified existence came into being in 1967, with the move to the BR shed at Didcot that had been closed in June 1965.

Since that time, the Society has grown beyond most imaginings, to become one of the 'Premier League' sites,

Below: The boiler glistens in the rain in October 1972 as an enthusiast peers at the motion for identification of other locomotives stamped thereon. Here restored to near its condition when new in 1889 as L&YR No 1008, it later became LMS 10621 (in 1923), then BR No 50621. In all, 210 members of Aspinall's Class '5' were built, and No 1008 spent much time at Normanton (Leeds) shed, from where the end came in 1954. It was then saved for the National Collection.

Bottom: Another saved for the nation was ex-LSWR No 120. A member of the 66-strong 'T9' 4-4-0 class, it was new in 1899. Seen on a sunny day in September 1970, the opportunity for a closer look as it stood next to the coaling stage was obviously being made the most of, including the tender vantage point. This veteran Drummond engine was deleted from BR's books at Eastleigh on 9 November 1961, and was returned to LSWR livery for restoration. *Both MJS*

despite its somewhat constrained nature. There have been many ambitions and achievements over the past 40-plus years, and neither shows any signs of lessening pace. 2010 has seen the steaming of No 6023 *King Edward II* – once considered a basket case – for the first time since 1962! Progress is continuing on creating 'new builds' of a 'County' 4-6-0, 'Star' 4-6-0 and steam Railmotor; there are plans for extension and development of the site; and agreement has been reached to move three of the 'Barry 10' – Nos 2861, 4115 and 5227 – to Didcot, for both short-term use of parts for the new builds and, longer term, full restoration of all three.

Alongside all these laudable aims and realisations, the Society has not lost sight of the importance of visitor numbers and

Top left: 1931-vintage No 5900 *Hinderton Hall*, a loco that has faded from sight at Didcot over recent years, here stands at Didcot blessed with low evening sunshine on 16 August 1991. Sent to Barry in March 1965 after withdrawal, it left its seaside retreat in 1971, was restored to steam in 1976, and has worked out on the main line.

Centre left: Between 1944 and 1949 Hawksworth produced a variant of the '5900' Class, known as the 'Modified Hall'. No 6998 *Burton Agnes Hall* actually appeared in BR days, in 1949, and had a very short life, being withdrawn in January 1966. Saved from the cutter's torch by private individuals, it has been based at Didcot for longer than it was in service!

Bottom left: What dreams are made of! It is highly unlikely that No 6106 would ever have had the opportunity of heading the 'Cambrian Coast Express', but on 23 September 1973 it can pretend! Another of the GWS's early acquisitions, it has been a further stalwart of the Didcot Centre. *All MJS*

 DIDCOT

has continuously developed the on-site experience, for young and old. New things keep appearing, vital for ongoing success, but without losing the ambience of an ex-BR engine shed – a case of careful evolution rather than revolution.

Opened on 7 August 1960 the Bluebell Railway became the first standard gauge steam-operated preserved railway in the world and, as such, blazed a trail for others to follow. Initially formed the previous year as the Lewes & East Grinstead Railway Preservation Society, with an aim of reopening the line from East Grinstead to Culver Junction on the Uckfield-Lewes line, which had closed in 1958, lack of finance and local support scuppered that idea, so the more restrained Sheffield

Top right: No 5572 stands in the pleasant evening sunshine of 16 August 1991. New from Swindon in 1929 – a Collett development of Churchward's design – it was the last but two of the class. Withdrawn in April 1962, it quickly found its way to Barry and did not leave until 1971, with an even longer gestation period from then to restoration in 1985.

Right: Seen on the same day, No 9466 was a mere youngster of just 12 years when withdrawn in 1964. Again there was a fairly swift removal to Barry, where it stayed for ten years until its salvation in 1975. Once more, it was not until 1985 that steam returned to its boiler.

Below: Way before Health & Safety regulations clamped down, a single rope served to keep back the public from the running line. On 23 September 1973 No 1466 gives rides in two handsomely turned-out carriages. New in 1936, as No 4866, it was withdrawn in 1963 and was protected from the trip to Barry by being privately purchased, becoming one of just four of the class to be saved. *All MJS*

One of the delights of the GWS headquarters at Didcot in former years was the annual 'night-time' occasion. With floodlights strategically placed around the site, photographers could indulge themselves with tripods and long shutter times for some stunning shots. The evening of 26 October 1991 has No 6024 *King Edward I* to the fore in the yard, gleaming and looking magnificent. The 'King' Class locomotives were rightly regarded as masters of their work and highly revered by enthusiasts, so it is perhaps sad that only three of the total of 31 have been preserved. The second of them to be back in steam, No 6024 had emerged from Swindon in June 1930, was fitted with a double chimney in March 1957, and ran a total of some 1,570,015 miles by the time it was 'retired' by BR. Over the past decade it has given countless enthusiasts and the travelling public delight when seen or experienced on the main line. *MJS*

Main picture: In this late-afternoon view of Sheffield Park shed yard on 18 April 1979, some of the variety of motive power available to the Bluebell Railway can be seen. To the left, 'USA' No 30064 looks smart in its lined green livery, with its non-UK design indicating its origin as a 1943 product of the US Transportation Corps. Acquired by the Southern Railway after the war, it was initially allocated the number 64 and used for shunting, especially at Southampton Docks. It left there in June 1963 and survived until the end of steam on BR(SR) in July 1967 at (mostly) Eastleigh. Preservation was almost immediate. To its right stands Maunsell 'U' Class 2-6-0 No 31618 (Brighton, 1928) and, on the far right, Bulleid's unrebuilt No 21C123 (February 1946), later to become No 34023 under BR. Initially incorrectly named *Blackmoor Vale,* this was corrected to the proper version – *Blackmore Vale* – in April 1950.

Bottom left: Showing what can be achieved by dedication to accurate recreation wherever possible, No 31263, as SE&CR No 263, poses as originally conceived. New from Ashford in 1905, as one of Wainwright's 'H' Class 0-4-4Ts, its long and well-travelled working life lasted until 27 January 1964.

Bottom right: Tucked away on a siding, another Wainwright design – 'P' Class 0-6-0T No 31027 of February 1910 – is in pseudo-SE&CR livery as No 27. It spent 18 months in France during the First World War, serving with the ROD. Behind stands another 'P', No 31178, also from February 1910, as SE&CR No 178. It was renumbered A178 (July 1924), 1178 (November 1931), S1178 (March 1948) and, finally, 31178 (May 1951). *All MJS*

1979 SHEFFIELD PARK

Park to Bluebell Halt (just short of Horsted Keynes) stretch was first leased and then bought from BR.

Being the precursor of any movement brings its own inherent troubles, from which other similar projects have gained knowledge, but the railway, now long known and loved by the highly attractive 'Bluebell Railway' name, has gradually overcome whatever has been before it and has developed and expanded over the past 50 years to become one of the UK's major attractions. A re-entry to East Grinstead station, to rejoin the main Network Rail system, has been creeping ever closer over recent times and is now in sight, with a presence at the station now awaiting the arrival of infrastructure and trains from the south. Imberhorne cutting has been the most recent stumbling block, infilled during the years of closure and now in the process of being rescued. Track

has been laid from East Grinstead and the summer of 2010 was to see the opening of a new platform for the railway there and running to the northern end of the former tip, over the reinstated viaduct.

Longer-term plans could be a return of trains to Ardingley, as the railway has purchased the trackbed from there to Horsted Keynes and has applied for planning permission to rebuild the Sheriff Mill viaduct, demolished in 1968. The remaining clearance of the tip waste could be by rail, over the new line to East Grinstead, and this would both speed up clearance and provide fresh photographic opportunities for enthusiasts. The company's workshops are also gaining in importance, with

restoration of the line's stock – with both Class 'Ps' returning in 2010 – and involvement in new builds. Though perhaps not receiving the press coverage applied to other such creations elsewhere in the UK, the 'Brighton Atlantic Project', based on the railway, is steadily gathering parts and materials, and the recreation of one of the iconic locos will be a day to be savoured. Elsewhere, the line has a fascinating collection of steam locomotives, large and small, ancient and (slightly more) modern.

Left: Yet more variety on this day in April 1979. Another youngster that suffered changes of demands under BR, No 80100 was just ten years old when withdrawn from Shrewsbury in September 1965. A swift move to Barry was then followed by 13 years of bombardment from the sea air, leading to the dilapidated condition as seen here. Again evidencing some of the variety on show, on the left are Nos 488 (BR No 30583) and 92240 (without smoke deflectors), and on the right LNWR No 2650 (BR No 58850). *MJS*

1982 SWANAGE

The Swanage Railway *(above)* had the seaside as an attraction but not high-profile railway coverage in the early days, compared to some, but it battled on regardless. Sometimes appearing painfully slow, the railway has steadily pushed its boundaries, with re-entry to the tourist honeypot of Corfe Castle being a milestone and, more recently, reconnection to the main railway network. On 28 July 1982 the boiler of 'Standard 4' 2-6-4T No 80078 is off the frames and the smokebox still looks in need of attention, but some TLC has already been lavished on firebox and boiler. This was another locomotive to suffer ten years at the seaside at Barry, before coming to the Isle of Purbeck in 1976. *MJS*

1987 BUXTON

Left: The condition of some locomotives rescued from Barry Docks certainly looked as though it would task the volunteers that were hopeful of restoration, and many would take much longer than originally thought or hoped. No 92219 looks decidedly weary in this view at Buxton on 12 July 1987, and such was its state that someone has obviously felt the need to chalk 'Do Not Cut' on the driving wheels! To Barry in 1965, immediately after withdrawal from Cardiff East Dock shed on 19 September, this last but one steam locomotive to be built at Swindon Works – new in February 1960 – spent 20 years in the sea air before removal to Buxton in 1986. *Ray Ruffell, Silver Link collection*

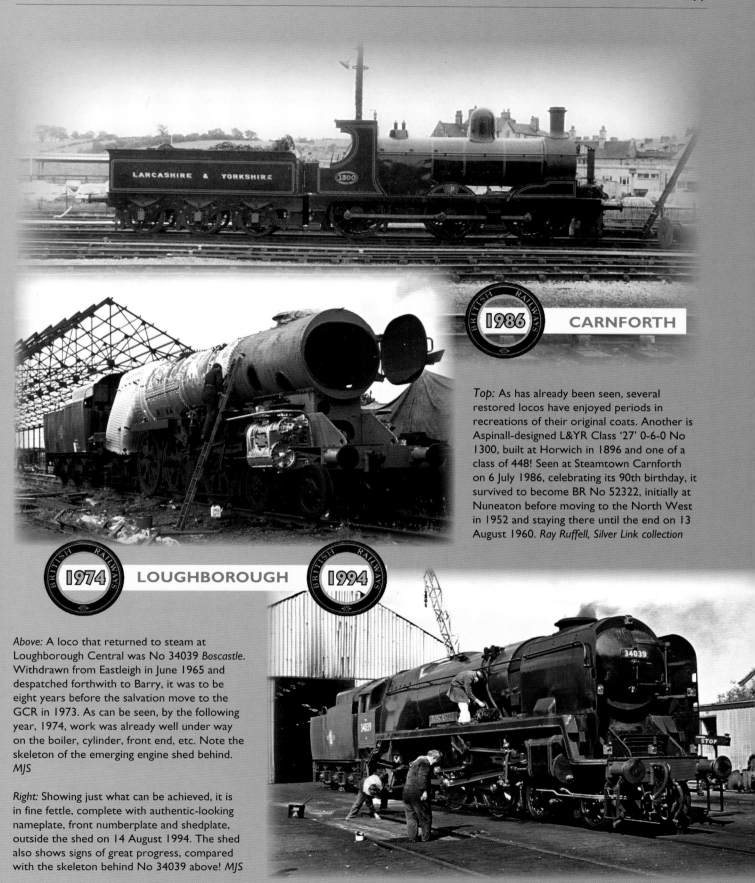

1986 CARNFORTH

Top: As has already been seen, several restored locos have enjoyed periods in recreations of their original coats. Another is Aspinall-designed L&YR Class '27' 0-6-0 No 1300, built at Horwich in 1896 and one of a class of 448! Seen at Steamtown Carnforth on 6 July 1986, celebrating its 90th birthday, it survived to become BR No 52322, initially at Nuneaton before moving to the North West in 1952 and staying there until the end on 13 August 1960. *Ray Ruffell, Silver Link collection*

1974 LOUGHBOROUGH 1994

Above: A loco that returned to steam at Loughborough Central was No 34039 *Boscastle*. Withdrawn from Eastleigh in June 1965 and despatched forthwith to Barry, it was to be eight years before the salvation move to the GCR in 1973. As can be seen, by the following year, 1974, work was already well under way on the boiler, cylinder, front end, etc. Note the skeleton of the emerging engine shed behind. *MJS*

Right: Showing just what can be achieved, it is in fine fettle, complete with authentic-looking nameplate, front numberplate and shedplate, outside the shed on 14 August 1994. The shed also shows signs of great progress, compared with the skeleton behind No 34039 above! *MJS*

Left: This view of No 71000 at Crewe South shed on 3 September 1967 is enough to break an enthusiast's heart and vividly shows some of the work needed to restore it; the right-hand cylinder has been stripped away, so restoration would necessitate the fabrication of a completely new one. *MJS*

Centre left: A quick repeat of the shot on page 44, showing the engine in rude health, climbing Camden Bank in 1957. *MJS collection*

Centre right: The Main Line Steam Trust, later to become the Great Central Railway heritage line, tackled one of its most onerous restoration feats in returning No 71000 *Duke of Gloucester* to steam. Not only is the engine one of the largest in the ex-BR fleet, it had

also been partly cannibalised following withdrawal in 1962, so the restorers faced a mountain when a life of only 8½ years may have led some to believe that the body would not be worn out. In 1974 dismantling has begun and the smokebox looks in reasonable condition, but the skeleton engine shed will not give the volunteers much in the way of shelter! *MJS*

Bottom: In its first run out on the main line on 7 April 1990, the 'Duke' finally has a chance to stretch its legs at the head of the Didcot-Derby and return section of Flying Scotsman Services' 'The Red Dragon' rail tour. Watched by incredibly few photographers, it accelerates away from Didcot and storms through Appleford station, past the mock-GWR 'Pagoda' waiting shelters. *MJS*

**CREWE SOUTH
CAMDEN BANK
LOUGHBOROUGH
APPLEFORD**

1957   1990

EARLY PRESERVED LINES

THE BLUEBELL RAILWAY

2008   **HORSTED KEYNES**

1985   **HORSTED KEYNES**

To be the first in anything is chancy and takes guts, determination, vision and, frequently, thick skin. The pitfalls are many, naysayers legion, and positive volunteers usually thin on the ground. Taking its name from the bluebells that inhabit the woodlands alongside the line, the original goal for this first attempt to preserve a standard gauge line was to save the whole of the ex-LB&SCR line from East Grinstead to Lewes, which had closed to Culver Junction at the southern end on 17 March 1958, and operate it as a commercial service. Progressively this proved impossible and

plans were perforce re-examined. Opening on 7 August 1960, and making its headquarters at Sheffield Park station, early stock was moved to the site via the Haywards Heath-Horsted Keynes branch, which was operational until 28 October 1963. From the start, a wide variety of motive power and other items began to congregate at Sheffield Park with, in the 21st century, in excess of 30 locomotives on hand, the oldest being ex-LB&SCR 'Terrier' No 72 *Fenchurch* dating from 1872.

More recently, eyes have been on the prize of re-entering East Grinstead station, and this has been tantalisingly close since the extension from Horsted Keynes to Kingscote in 1994 and clearance of the 'tip' material in the cutting between Imberhorne Lane and Hill Place bridges, which began in 2008. At the same time, steps have been taken to prepare the site at East Grinstead and the future return looks ever closer.

Top: The Bluebell Railway is undoubtedly one of the best in recreating scenes from the past. On 28 March 2008 No 1638, in 'Southern' livery, departs from Horsted Keynes with a decidedly mixed SR goods train heading for Kingscote. *Matt Allen*

Left: At Horsted Keynes in 1985 'Standard 4' No 80064 has a clear road and waits for the doors to be closed to restart its journey. One of your authors was working at that time for the well-known and respected publishing firm of Patrick Stephens Ltd (PSL) and was attending The Booksellers Association national conference in nearby Brighton – or should that read 'should have been attending...'? PSL will be well known to many readers as publishers of several fine railway titles over the years, and this visit to the Bluebell Railway was of course entirely in the line of business! *Peter Townsend*

1967   BUCKFASTLEIGH

1967   BUCKFASTLEIGH

On the same hot summer's day, No 4555 stands in Buckfastleigh station, smartly turned out, with headlamps in place and carriage doors open for potential traffic, but the engine is not in steam and no one is going anywhere! Of the 14 members of the class saved for further work on heritage lines, this is the oldest, emerging from Swindon Works in 1924, with the original straight-topped side tanks. Like No 1420, No 4555 travelled widely, with tenures

Above: Looking towards Ashburton on 22 August 1967, in the days before construction on the A38 severed the link, No 1420 stands at Buckfastleigh with its Auto coach, in all aspects appearing to be ready to push-pull along a branch line. Built at Swindon in 1933 as No 4820, it plied its trade in a variety of areas, from South Wales to Worcester, by way of Oxford, Slough, Plymouth and Hereford. Following disposal by BR in November 1964, it was successfully acquired for preservation, predominantly on the SDR.

at Machynlleth, Westbury, Newton Abbot, St Blazey and Plymouth (Laira). Also like No 1420, it was sold by BR direct into preservation, following withdrawal on 30 November 1963. *Both MJS*

Originally born as the Dart Valley Railway, formally opening on 5 April 1969 – with ex-GWR 0-6-0PT No 6412 in steam – the South Devon Railway Trust took over the running of the line as from 1 January 1991. It has also been called the 'Primrose Line'. After the line had been closed by BR on 7 September 1962, a group of businessmen announced their intention to run it as a tourist line, and in 1965 the first rolling stock arrived.

The current line runs for 6¾ miles from Totnes (Littlehempston) – which now boasts a footbridge to access the main-line station – to Buckfastleigh, but in the early days the railway also had access to Ashburton, to the north of Buckfastleigh station, where it had established its headquarters. Sadly, this 2-mile stretch from Buckfastleigh

Main picture: Bearing in mind that the trip to Ashburton is no longer available to us and unlikely ever to be, despite aspirations locally, we invite you to savour this view of No 1450 at that terminus in 1970. This rarely seen wider aspect shows an Auto coach outside the goods shed, the overall cover for the terminus platform and the delightful GWR water tank – a wonderful portrait and a superb evocation for a modeller of GWR operation. *David Richards*

THE SOUTH DEVON RAILWAY

to Ashburton was lost in 1971 with the widening of the A38 trunk road. The first rolling stock – GWR locomotives 4555 and 3205 and four BR(W) auto-trailers – arrived on 2 October 1965, and since then the number and variety of motive power and stock has increased. Ironically, the line was opened in 1969 by Dr Beeching, although this was not one of those condemned on his list!

The railway gives a superb evocation of a typical West Country branch line, with a predominantly period air, despite some more modern stock. The delightful Dart valley and the meandering River Dart are associated attractions, with butterflies and otters completing the scene, and the whole is a paradise for photographers on a fine sunny day. The terminus at Ashburton, with its overall train shed, goods shed, water tower, etc, would have been a fantastic template for modellers, but the rest of the SDR does its best to compensate.

1967 **ASHBURTON**

BRESSINGHAM STEAM MUSEUM

A somewhat surprising preservation centre is the private steam museum, gardens and garden centre set in the grounds of Bressingham Hall in Norfolk. Established by Alan Bloom MBE and eventually protected by a Trust in his name, it has housed a number of famous ex-BR locomotives over time, including Nos 46100 *Royal Scot*, 46233 *Duchess of Sutherland*, 70013 *Oliver Cromwell*, GNR 990 *Henry Oakley*, LT&SR No 80 *Thundersley*, LSWR 102 *Granville* and LB&SCR 662 *Martello*. There is also a wide variety of other steam items in the collection.

Below: Bressingham was in many ways unique in railway preservation, accommodating within a relatively small area railways of differing gauges, a circular route and a fairground! It also entombed high-profile ex-BR locomotives, such as the famed *Royal Scot*. Devoid of its front number, it is in its LMS red coat and in steam on 16 September 1973, giving rides in the cab. *MJS*

BRESSINGHAM

DINTING

Right: Dinting was another small, and sadly short-lived and missed, preservation site, and it too had celebrity locos on site over time. Certainly No 45596 *Bahamas* is in this category, and looks as if it is being given a coat of whitewash – presumably undercoat for a repaint – on 31 July 1988. New on 12 January 1935 from Queens Park Works, Glasgow, at a cost of £5,866, it was named on 8 June the following year. It was given a double chimney in May 1961 at Crewe and had completed about 1,300,000 miles at withdrawal, which came on 13 August 1966. *Ray Ruffell, Silver Link collection*

THE GREAT CENTRAL RAILWAY

Initially the Main Line Preservation Group, with laudable aims to restore the old GCR from Nottingham to Leicester, reality soon set in and the parameters were redrawn. Concentrating on Loughborough station as its headquarters, the first aim was to consolidate presence on this site and to begin regaining the path southwards as soon and as fast as possible, this being the only ex-BR main line that was to be saved.

One of the greatest and most controversial of Dr Beeching's cuts – and arguably the greatest folly – the line ceased as a through route from September 1966, with a rump operating thereafter with DMUs between Rugby Central and Nottingham Victoria until 1969. Final closure of the line brought together those keen to prevent disappearance of the railway and a lease was granted for the station, buildings and most of the trackbed at Loughborough in 1970. The intention throughout was for double-track running, but early years had to be satisfied with single track as the pressures of renovating Loughborough station, edging south with track and attracting visitors took their toll. And the problems did not end there. As 'Black 5' No 5231 was hauling the first train to Quorn on 30 September 1973, BR was ripping up the track further south, all the way to Birstall!

Happily, since then the railway has overcome many near fatal obstacles – not least financial – to create that double-track experience and to reach Leicester, albeit only just, with the new Leicester North station being just yards inside the city boundary! Over years the railway has extended its appeal as well as its track and has developed into a First Division attraction, with aspirations to regain the route north, crossing over the Midland Main Line on the way, as in days of yore.

Top: The headboard reinforces where we are! On 30 April 1988 No 6990 *Witherslack Hall* accelerates away from Loughborough Central with 'The Great Central Limited' dining train. A 1948 Swindon product, its first port of call was Old Oak Common, where it stayed until November

1988 LOUGHBOROUGH

1963, apart from two years at Oxford. Bristol was then its home until the end of steam on the Western Region at the end of 1965. At Barry from 1966, departure came nine years later, with a further 11 years before restoration at the GCR in 1986.

Left: Though still in the early years of the MLST/GCR, progress and transformation is already in hand at Loughborough in April 1973. Remedial work is being applied to the steps down to the platform, and the platform itself is being re-laid, while on the sole track on this side 'Black 5' No 5231 is gleaming and has obviously been well looked after. New in 1936, it was another of the class to survive until the end of steam on BR in August 1968, having served at a wide array of sheds and districts within the LMS/BR(MR) system. *Both MJS*

1973 LOUGHBOROUGH

The Midland Railway Centre is not just a centre for preserved and preservation of railway locomotives and/or artefacts, but is, in addition, a massive museum and country park, with excellent photographic opportunities such as when trains cross the delightful Butterley Reservoir.

While Didcot aimed at preserving the GWR and Bluebell the SR, the MRC was unashamedly Midland and its antecedents. Situated midway on the west-east MR branch from Ambergate to Pye Bridge, closed as a through route on 11 September 1961 and totally in 1968, in an area of industrial dereliction, initial thoughts in 1969 saw a group of enthusiasts in tandem with Derbyshire County Council and Derby Corporation plan for a museum, but these two partners had to withdraw through financial constraints. Undeterred, the Midland Railway Company Ltd was formed on 20 February 1973 – later changed to the Midland Railway Trust – with headquarters at Butterley and a museum site

at Swanwick. Moving the old station building at Whitwell to Butterley to replace the original, which had been demolished, a steam open day was held in 1975. The first passenger trains finally ran in 1981. Later developments were to see Ais Gill, Kettering and Kilby Bridge signal boxes and Syston station building transferred to the site, and the expansion of line and services.

THE MIDLAND RAILWAY CENTRE

The MRC currently boasts around 30 main-line locomotives, both steam and diesel, together with DMUs, more than 20 industrial locos, again steam and diesel, and in excess of 100 items of rolling stock. A visit there will therefore provide much to satisfy and entertain. Again there are plans to extend further, to Pye Bridge and a connection with the Network Rail Erewash Valley line, which will further extend the centre's appeal.

Though built by R. Stephenson & Co in 1925 to a Fowler design for the Somerset & Dorset Railway, that line was part owned by the Midland Railway, so it is fitting to see this locomotive preserved at the Midland Railway Centre. Initially S&DJR No 89, then 9679, it is seen here in its last LMS guise as it leaves Butterley on 15 July 1984. It became No 53809 under BR, stayed at Bath (Green Park) shed and became surplus in July 1964 when other motive power was shipped in to the S&DJR. *MJS*

BUTTERLEY

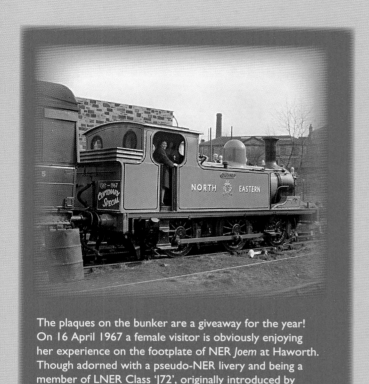

The plaques on the bunker are a giveaway for the year! On 16 April 1967 a female visitor is obviously enjoying her experience on the footplate of NER *Joem* at Haworth. Though adorned with a pseudo-NER livery and being a member of LNER Class 'J72', originally introduced by Worsdell from 1898, this loco was from a batch of 28 built by BR between 1949 and 1951! Numbered 69023, it became 'Departmental No 59' on 19 December 1964 and was withdrawn on 8 October 1966. Happily, preservation beckoned via ICI Ltd at Wilton, Middlesbrough.

THE KEIGHLEY & WORTH VALLEY RAILWAY

The Keighley & Worth Valley Railway was to add yet another facet to the still fledgling but ever-expanding heritage railway movement of the 1960s, with aspirations to reopen and run a complete branch! In this case, the branch was 'only' 4¾ miles but the original had been constructed due to local community demands and this local support was still there at the end. Even before the railway ceased operations on 31 December 1961 a preservation society was formed. Six years of hard work passed in negotiations with BR and other interested parties, together with necessary spade work on the ground, but financial agreements were made and paid and in 1965 stock began to arrive. This further encouraged existing supporters and brought new ones to the project. Formal reopening was on 29 June 1968.

The big break for the railway, of course, was the opting of BBC TV to use the line in an adaptation of E. Nesbit's *The Railway Children*. There followed the iconic and much-loved film version, famously directed by Lionel Jeffries and starring Jenny Agutter (playing the role of Roberta as in the BBC

HAWORTH

version), Sally Thomsett, Dinah Sheridan and Bernard Cribbins. The popularity of this and the book still waves a magic wand over the railway, but at the time it encouraged loco-owners to offer their prize possessions, again to the railway's benefit. It was thus the first railway to run a complete line; the first to buy a loco from Dai Woodham's Barry scrapyard; the first to steam a National Collection engine (No 42700); and the first to have four gas-lit stations for added realism.

Left: We have seen No 52044 previously, in pre- and post-restoration to BR condition, on page 84, but here it is at a slightly earlier period, in the initial incarnation on the K&WVR. On 16 April 1967 it stands as L&YR No 957 (its pre-1923 condition) in Haworth's yard, looking spick and span and receiving close attention. *Both Ray Ruffell, Silver Link collection*

PEAK RAIL

Peak Rail has another slant on the preservation story, in that it has seen a complete change of location. Originating at Buxton in 1975, on the site of the erstwhile Midland Railway side of the town's station, the site was cramped and proposals to 'break out' by a bridge to the existing BR line came to nothing. The Buxton Steam Centre basically inhabited the old goods shed and had 300 yards of 'running line', together with sidings and a signal box. Potential

1987   BUXTON

Above: The Peak Rail group has had some turbulent times, not least with its original site at Buxton. In slightly happier times, on 12 July 1987, a selection of industrial locos occupies the main 'running lines', including one giving rides, with more stock in the sidings to the right. *Ray Ruffell, Silver link collection*

Right: Following the purchase of the old Rewley Road, Oxford, station building and its re-erection at Quainton Road, the BRC has made great strides in achievement and customer attraction. Earlier times saw a different state of affairs, when, on 11 May 1982, No 7200 has only recently arrived from Barry after a 17-year exposure to the elements there. *MJS*

was very limited, so a move to the other end of Derbyshire came in 1991, with the reopening of a line between Matlock and Darley Dale. Subsequent extension towards Rowsley and the hope of rejoining the network at Matlock, together with sights set on Bakewell, spur on the volunteers and encourage visitors.

THE BUCKINGHAMSHIRE RAILWAY CENTRE

Seemingly 'in the middle of nowhere', with the Quainton Road station site bisected by Network Rail tracks and no connections or regular trains, and a very limited length of operational line, the BRC faces an uphill struggle for visitors against the other, mightier sites around the country.

Predominantly a museum, with connections to 'Metro-land' so beloved of Sir John Betjeman, it was given a fillip in 2002 with the piece-by-piece rebuilding of the closed 1851 Rewley Road, Oxford, station building, which was an attraction in itself and an 'overnight' purpose-built museum facility.

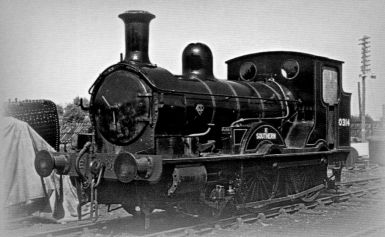

Left: On the same day, BR No 30585 is in much fitter condition, painted to represent post-1923 Southern Railway No E0314. Out of 85 of the Beattie 2-4-0 'Well Tanks' built from 1863, only two survive, both due to their use on the china clay traffic over the restricted Wenford Bridge branch in Cornwall. Withdrawal from there came in January 1963. *MJS*

1982   QUAINTON ROAD

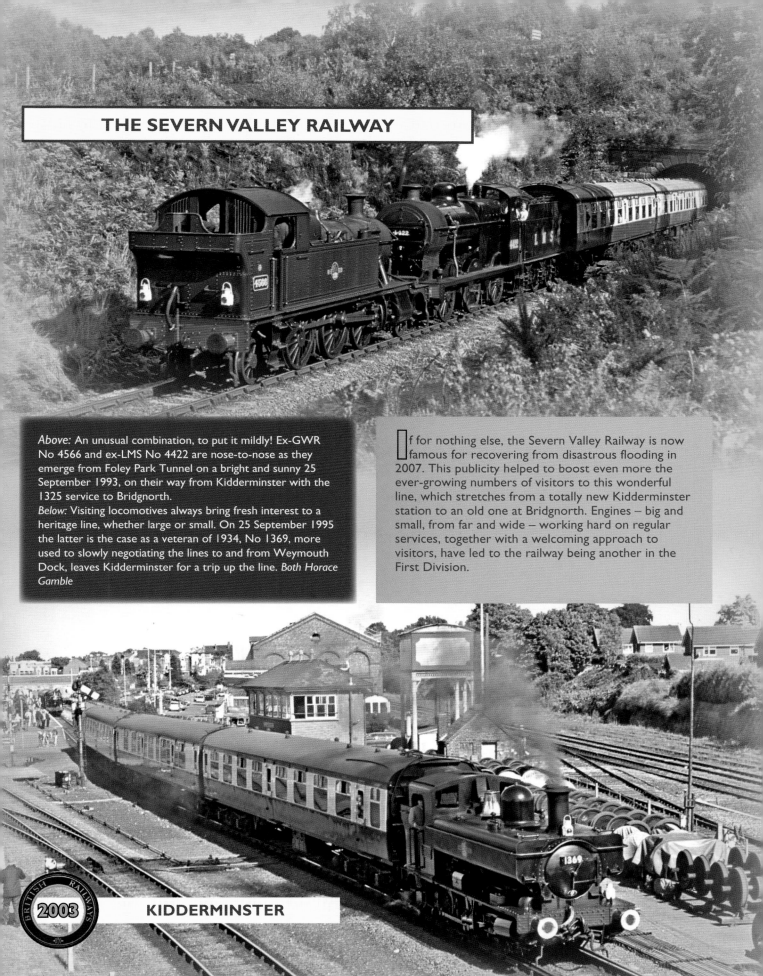

THE SEVERN VALLEY RAILWAY

Above: An unusual combination, to put it mildly! Ex-GWR No 4566 and ex-LMS No 4422 are nose-to-nose as they emerge from Foley Park Tunnel on a bright and sunny 25 September 1993, on their way from Kidderminster with the 1325 service to Bridgnorth.

Below: Visiting locomotives always bring fresh interest to a heritage line, whether large or small. On 25 September 1995 the latter is the case as a veteran of 1934, No 1369, more used to slowly negotiating the lines to and from Weymouth Dock, leaves Kidderminster for a trip up the line. *Both Horace Gamble*

If for nothing else, the Severn Valley Railway is now famous for recovering from disastrous flooding in 2007. This publicity helped to boost even more the ever-growing numbers of visitors to this wonderful line, which stretches from a totally new Kidderminster station to an old one at Bridgnorth. Engines – big and small, from far and wide – working hard on regular services, together with a welcoming approach to visitors, have led to the railway being another in the First Division.

2003

KIDDERMINSTER

Below: First, an apology for the quality, due to rapidly fading light combined with the vagaries of the Agfa slide emulsion of the time, but the capture of a rare outing of a 'Castle' on the Midland Main Line is our justification. On 27 March 1965 No 7029 *Clun Castle* speeds south at Thurmaston, 4 miles to the north of Leicester, with 1X20, the Ian Allan 'Lickey & Midlands Railtour', which it hauled from Paddington and back with a short break at Nottingham, by way of Bromsgrove, Derby, Leicester, Northampton and High Wycombe. Notice that despite the superb vantage point alongside the line, there are few others there to witness the event. *MJS*

Below right inset: Still at Thurmaston, but 200 yards further south, No 4472 *Flying Scotsman* approaches your photographer, who is in glorious isolation on 10 September 1966! The Gainsborough Model Railway Society's 'Farnborough Flyer' rail tour ran from Doncaster to Farnborough and back, out via the Midland Main Line and Feltham East Junction and back via Kew and Acton Wells Junction. Emerging from Doncaster in 1923 as LNER No 1472, it was displayed at the British Empire Exhibition at Wembley the following year, renumbered to 4472, and in 1934 became the first locomotive to officially reach 100mph. Following the end of its BR service in 1963, as No 60103, it was privately purchased by Alan Pegler. Its subsequent history has been well documented. *MJS*

1965   THURMASTON   1966

MAIN LINE STEAM RETURNS 1968 - 1990

As we have seen, Saturday 11 August 1968 was a milestone date in the UK's railway calendar and was potentially a 'double whammy'. For not only did this bring the curtain down on steam operation as a normal factor of BR's day-to-day workings, but it also promised to be the death knell of steam on the main lines. With effect from the end of October of that year, an edict was issued that unilaterally banned steam on the main line thenceforward, with just one exception. Prior to that, the occasional run was enjoyed by privately owned locos, but all that nonsense was to stop. The one exception was *Flying Scotsman,* as owner Alan Pegler was the proud possessor of a contract to allow working on the main line until 1972! Even engines from the National Collection were included in the ban, and the future for steam enthusiasts looked very dark indeed.

The last main-line run by *Scotsman* was on 14 September 1969, just before its ill-fated trip to the USA, and this was therefore the barren steam situation into the early 1970s, until...

Almost exactly three years after the bombshell announcement, the ice was broken by another iconic locomotive. On 2 October 1971 No 6000 *King George V* emerged from its incarceration in the Hereford base of Bulmer's Cider to run to Tyseley, via Severn Tunnel Junction, Oxford and Banbury, with a rake of the company's Pullman stock in tow. Two days later it was travelling from Birmingham (Moor Street) back to Hereford by way of Kensington (Olympia) and Swindon! Achieved by the persuasive skills of Peter Prior, Bulmer's MD, it was intended to be a 'one-off', but such was the success and the public demands for more that the genie was out of the bottle.

Opposite left: Kings of the system back home at Swindon.

(top) The iconic class leader, No 6000 *King George V*, gently reverses through the station on 9 May 1987, watched by some startled members of the public, in the midst of the 'Severn-Wye Express' movements! Proudly displaying the bell donated to it at the Baltimore & Ohio Railroad centenary exhibition in September 1927 and wearing a Hereford (85C) shedplate, in recognition of once being resident at Bulmer's Cider plant there in the early days of preservation, it later became a static exhibit inside the STEAM Museum, situated in part of the old Swindon Works, out of the picture to the left.

Main picture Seen at Didcot on page 91, No 6024 *King Edward I* is here out on the main line on 9 September 1991 with a private charter, hauling a distinctly mixed rake of coaching stock across the junction for the Gloucester line, including Pullmans and an appallingly liveried support coach immediately behind the tender!

Above: The 1930-built 'King' is again seen on the route to Gloucester, as it accelerates away from the station on the outskirts of Swindon. With a BR-dictated headlamp alongside the standard versions, No 6024 works hard up the slope with 'The Red Dragon' of 30 January 1994, another private charter. Fitted with a double chimney in March 1957, it completed 1,570,015 miles in BR service and has added many more to that since preservation. *All MJS*

1987   SWINDON   1994

Initially, the powers that be responded negatively to calls for further exploits, citing such problems as lack of watering facilities since the end of steam on the main line, fewer crews experienced with either locos or routes, coal supplies and the interruption to scheduled services. However, a change of BR Chairman in 1972 brought an equal change of approach, and through new man Richard Marsh five secondary routes were given authorisation – Newcastle-Carlisle, Carnforth-Barrow, York-Scarborough, Shrewsbury-Newport and Birmingham (Moor Street)-Didcot. As the year wore on some 23 engines were given approval, together with their home depots, and on 10 June No 7029 *Clun Castle* was stretching its legs once more, on a Moor Street-Didcot-Hereford turn.

1983

STOKE BANK

Main picture: We now have a close-up of *Flying Scotsman*, working hard to catch up time on Stoke Bank on 27 February 1983 while working the SLOA's 'The Flying Scotsman Pullman', which it hauled from Peterborough to York. When purchased by Alan Pegler (see page 107), it had been fitted with a double chimney and German Federal Railways-style smoke deflectors, and he soon set about his attempt to return it to original LNER condition. 1968 saw it supplied with a second tender, to assist with a non-stop King's Cross-Edinburgh run, as steam had long since disappeared from the ECML and there were no watering facilities remaining on the route. Undertaking many tours over the years, perhaps one of the most eventful was that to the USA in 1969, where it was fitted with cowcatcher, buckeye couplings, a bell, air brakes and a high-intensity headlamp! This tour and other matters bankrupted Alan Pegler in 1972 and William McAlpine stepped in to save the iconic engine from its incarceration in San Francisco in 1973.

Below: Another view of No 4472 at Thurmaston, this time on 29 May 1965, some 15 months earlier than when seen on page 107. At the same location as *Clun Castle* on page 106, there are now many more 'worshippers' present to witness the passing of the RCTS (East Midlands Branch) 10-coach 'East Midlander No 8 Rail Tour'. Originating at Nottingham Midland, the tour was bang on time when photographed, and Clapham Junction was reached 14 minutes early! The return was via Swindon and the Lickey Incline, and arrival at Nottingham was just 6 minutes late! A highly creditable achievement. *Both MJS*

1965

THURMASTON

Of all the many designs of motive power over the years, perhaps the most graceful and aesthetically pleasing was Gresley's 'A4'. Happily six have been preserved, although two not in the UK! In the mid-1980s BR ran steam specials from Marylebone to Stratford-upon-Avon at weekends, to encourage people back onto the railway network and provide a 'grand day out'. On 3 February 1985 No 4498 *Sir Nigel Gresley* – in garter blue livery – pauses at Beaconsfield station to pick up passengers bound for Stratford. *MJS*

The following week saw 'A4' No 4498 *Sir Nigel Gresley* between Newcastle and Carlisle. The following year further routes were authorised and May saw No 92203 on ex-Southern metals in connection with an Eastleigh Works Open Day, and 1974 saw Nos 6998 *Burton Agnes Hall* and 7808 *Cookham Manor* with a rake of GWR coaches!

Thereafter, all manner of events happened: locos for S&D150 at Shildon on the main line; No 790 *Hardwicke* double-heading with No 92220 *Evening Star* from Leeds to York; No 4771

Green Arrow over the Settle and Carlisle route in 1978; and even reinstallation by BR of a turntable at Scarborough! The door was now well and truly open and over subsequent years the number

1985   BEACONSFIELD

and variety of locomotives out on the nation's main-line routes has grown almost exponentially, to the extent that by the first decade of the 21st century there are many occasions where several charter trains are running on the same day, and we now even have multi-day tours covering the length and breadth of the UK with a variety of different locomotives. Someone with a 40-year 'flash forward' in 1968 would doubtless not have believed their eyes!

As well as BR and organisations such as railway societies arranging rail tours, other one-off specials also appeared periodically. On 1 August 1984 Wilson & Co's brewery of Monsall Road in Manchester celebrated 150 years of production by operating a single-coach tour of the local railways for invited guests. It was hauled by the comparatively young, 1888-vintage LNWR 'Coal Tank' No 1054 (BR No 58926) and the train is seen arriving at Manchester (Victoria). Numbered 7799 by the LMS in 1923, it was initially withdrawn in January 1939, but reinstated in December 1940 in connection with wartime needs! After withdrawal by BR on 1 November 1958, it was purchased by J. M. Dunn, former shedmaster at Bangor. It can now be seen on the K&WVR. *MJS*

1984 MANCHESTER (Victoria)

Another of the tours from Marylebone, this time an evening one, is captured as 'Merchant Navy' No 35028 *Clan Line* bursts from Wooburn Moor Tunnel, on the southern outskirts of High Wycombe, on 30 April 1985. Masquerading as the 'Golden Arrow' luxury train, which it might have hauled between London and Dover, it carries the full regalia – headboard, British and French flags, golden arrows on the smoke deflectors and polished buffers. *MJS*

Below: In BR days, this view would have been virtually impossible, but since the advent of private tour operators using restored steam locomotives on the main line, sights such as this of SR No 777 (BR No 30777) *Sir Lamiel* are not so outlandish. Making a welcome change to the normal fare on offer, the 'King Arthur' pauses at Llandudno Junction on 30 July 1991 at the head of the 'North Wales Coast Express'. Another from the National Collection, No 777 was delivered from North British's Glasgow workshops in June 1925, one of a class of 54 4-6-0s designed by Maunsell and named after the Knights of the Round Table. A servant of many parts of the Southern Railway empire, it was dispensed with on 9 November 1961, from Basingstoke shed. *MJS*

LLANDUDNO JUNCTION

Seen from high on top of a multi-storey car park on 16 November 1985, 'West Country' No 34092 *City of Wells* storms north out of High Wycombe with yet another Marylebone to Stratford-upon-Avon day excursion. Despite the very dull weather on this morning, the combination of plenty of steam and the original 'air-smoothed' Bulleid design makes for a pleasing spectacle. New on 30 August 1949 from Brighton Works and named on 25 November (just *Wells* until 1 March 1950), it served just two homes

1985   HIGH WYCOMBE

BRITISH RAILWAYS

– Stewarts Lane and Salisbury – before withdrawal on 21 December 1964. This perhaps explains why it had the second lowest mileage of the class at the end – just 502,864 miles. It languished at Barry Docks from March 1965 to October 1971, after which it was transported to the K&WVR. Following restoration, it was fitted with a Giesl ejector in 1985. *MJS*

Below: We previously saw Fort William in BR steam days on page 53; now we are there not in BR steam days but in more recent times with the 'West Highlander'. This service was introduced by British Rail in 1984, bringing a regular steam service back to the stunningly beautiful line to Mallaig, albeit for a limited period each year. The service, now known as 'The Jacobite', and operated by West Coast Railways and continues to operate today. LMS Class 5 4-6-0 No 45407, here sporting the LMS number 5407, was built by Armstrong Whitworth in 1937. Having been withdrawn from Lostock Hall at the end of steam in 1968, the loco was purchased for preservation and today is based at the East Lancashire Railway. *Brian Grant*

1990   **FORT WILLIAM**

Another innovation over the years has been the occasional 'Steam on the Met' junketings, where passengers are given the opportunity to travel behind visiting steam locomotives, or behind ancient Metropolitan Railway electric loco *Sarah Siddons*, over the Metropolitan Underground system from London to Amersham and/or Watford. On 22 July 1990 'Standard' Class 4 2-6-4T No 80080 provides a black contrast to the Network SouthEast-liveried coaches behind it as it steams through Chorleywood station in weak sunshine en route to Amersham. Constructed at Brighton Works in March 1954, No 80080 was one of 155 class members designed for suburban and semi-express passenger work, based on the existing LMS series of 2-6-4Ts from Stanier and Fairburn. *MJS*

1990   **CHORLEY WOOD**

PRESERVED LINES
FROM STRENGTH TO STRENGTH

THE DEAN FOREST RAILWAY

Right: At precisely 10.52 and 41 seconds the Norchard signalman collects the token from the crew of Class '5700' 0-6-0PT No 9681 pulling in to the lower-level platform at Norchard. The Dean Forest Railway has grown progressively over the years since the preservation society formed in 1970 held its first open day in October 1971. Originally based at Parkend, in 1974 the society purchased land next to the freight branch at Norchard, then still open, and over the ensuing years has reopened the line from Lydney back to the original base at Parkend. Plans for further extension through the forest make this very much a line to keep track of! A visit is highly recommended if you have not yet explored this very picturesque area of the country. *PT*

2006 NORCHARD (Low Level)

Right: The AVR is one of the more recent railways trying to break out of its original restrictions and grow. On 14 December 1997 the next target is a halt closer to Bath, as 'M7' No 30053 has just arrived from Oldland Common, the northern extent of the line at this time. Built at Nine Elms Works in 1905, it has become another travelling ambassador for our steam heritage, and has probably been a little less restricted in destinations than in its mostly Eastleigh-Brighton axis in BR days. *MJS*

THE AVON VALLEY RAILWAY

1997 BITTON

THE LLANGOLLEN RAILWAY

2000   BRITISH RAILWAYS

CARROG

Over the years, with the gradual extension of the running line from its base at Llangollen, the railway has developed itself into one of the leading heritage lines. In what could be a representation of a holidaymakers' train on its way to the seaside, No 44806 drifts into Carrog station on 16 July 2000. Currently the terminus, a further extension, to Corwen, is the next goal. *MJS*

Opposite: Back at base, ex-LMS 'Jinty' No 7298 pauses for a drink at Llangollen on 16 November 1991. A Bletchley incumbent for many years, its one and only move under BR was to Sutton Oak shed on 11 September 1954, from where the end came on the last day of 1966. Moving to Barry Docks the following year, it was to see seven years by the sea before salvation, and a return to steam at Llangollen in 1979. Retaining much of the original GWR railway infrastructure, the station has real character for the visitor. *Ray Ruffell, Silver Link collection*

7298

BRITISH RAILWAYS 1991

LLANGOLLEN

The ESR has been faced with and forced to overcome the restrictions of a short running line, but has nevertheless managed to acquire a reputation for visitor appeal. Loans from other railways help and, on 26 September 2004, No 41312 adds to the variety as it enters Cranmore station in company with the railway's own pseudo-USA tank, prior to working a train to Mendip Vale, the western terminus.

THE BODMIN & WENFORD RAILWAY

Below: Another line that is currently only able to run a limited distance, the B&WR has hopes of extending westwards towards Wadebridge and Padstow. Bodmin General is a terminus station in the middle of the present route, and is seen here welcoming No 4247 on 16 June 2008 with the 1425 service from Boscarne Junction. *Both MJS*

THE EAST SOMERSET RAILWAY

2004 CRANMORE

2008 BODMIN GENERAL

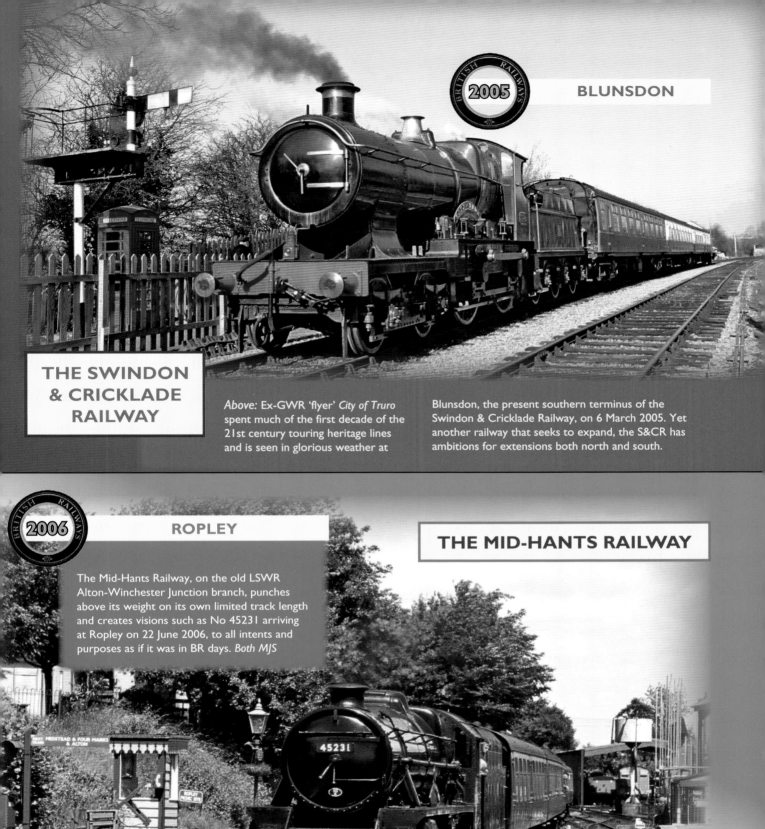

2005

BLUNSDON

THE SWINDON & CRICKLADE RAILWAY

Above: Ex-GWR 'flyer' *City of Truro* spent much of the first decade of the 21st century touring heritage lines and is seen in glorious weather at

Blunsdon, the present southern terminus of the Swindon & Cricklade Railway, on 6 March 2005. Yet another railway that seeks to expand, the S&CR has ambitions for extensions both north and south.

2006

ROPLEY

THE MID-HANTS RAILWAY

The Mid-Hants Railway, on the old LSWR Alton-Winchester Junction branch, punches above its weight on its own limited track length and creates visions such as No 45231 arriving at Ropley on 22 June 2006, to all intents and purposes as if it was in BR days. *Both MJS*

A trio of delights on the GCR.

Right: Fire and frost at Loughborough on 29 December 1995. Low temperatures retain the frost on the telegraph wires and lineside grass and create a wonderfully powerful effect from both smoke and steam escaping from No 46229 *Duchess of Hamilton* as it leaves Loughborough in the early morning.

Bottom right: Exactly two years earlier – bar one day! – the white stuff is again surrounding the railway, but this time as snow. Another bitterly cold day sees No 4498 (BR No 60007) *Sir Nigel Gresley* put its shoulder to the wheel as it gathers speed on the exit from Loughborough Central station on 28 December 1993. The fireman keeps a wary eye on your photographer! *Both MJS*

THE GREAT CENTRAL RAILWAY

Below: In the reckoning for one of the smallest BR locos, No 68088 stands alongside Rothley station on 22 February 1992. Classified 'Y7' by the LNER, this ex-NER Class 'H' Worsdell-design 0-4-0T is one of 24 constructed and was actually released from Darlington Works in 1923, numbered LNER 985. Originally with dumb buffers, the more standard type were fitted in the 1930s, and from 1943 to 1952 the locomotive shunted the yards at Stratford shed, with coal piled on the tank tops, as it was without a bunker behind the cab. Sold to the NCB in 1952, it worked at Bentinck Colliery until 1964, when it was purchased by the Y7 Society. *Ray Ruffell, Silver Link collection*

1995 LOUGHBOROUGH

1992 ROTHLEY

LOUGHBOROUGH 1994

THE STRATHSPEY RAILWAY

We have seen two of the Scottish preserved locos (see page 58); we now have a third, this time alive and kicking, at Boat of Garten. Great North of Scotland Railway Class 'F' No 49, latterly LNER 'D40' Class 4-4-0 No 2277 *Gordon Highlander*, was built by the North British Locomotive Co in 1920 to Heywood's development of the original Pickersgill design of 1899. Seen arriving at Boat of Garten with a two-coach train and carrying BR number 62277, it came into British Railways stock at Ferryhill (Aberdeen) shed but fairly smartly moved to Keith in July 1951, where it ended its working life on 5 July 1958, being the last of its class to be withdrawn. Restored by British Railways to GNoS livery as No 49 (inaccurately, the purists would argue, as it would have been in the later black livery when it entered service), it returned to service for special trains in 1959. After several years of sterling service, the fine old lady was retired once again to the safe keeping of the Glasgow Museum of Transport. *MJS collection*

1959

BOAT OF GARTEN

1979   **AVIEMORE**

Below: A much more modern motive power representative present and active on the Strathspey Railway in 1979 was ex-LMS 'Black 5' No 5025, seen here at Aviemore waiting to form the 1440 train to Boat of Garten. In true 'mixed-traffic' style, the 'Black 5s' seemingly went everywhere and many moved home on several occasions, but this particular example – which survived until the end of steam on BR – served just four sheds in the final 20 years of life, although at either end of the WCML (Willesden and Carlisle) up to 1963. *Ray Ruffell, Silver Link collection*

THE NORTH YORK MOORS RAILWAY

Another railway that has carved a strong niche in the heritage railway market, the NYMR has managed to both create interest within its existing confines and break out onto the Network Rail line at the northern end, with hopes of reinstating the currently severed link south. Visiting engines or those unusual for the location are a vital revenue source here as elsewhere, and 'Schools' No 30926 *Repton* would certainly not have been seen here in BR days. Snapped at Grosmont on 23 July 1994, it is impatient to begin the run to Pickering. Built at Eastleigh in 1934, it was one of 40 of these 4-4-0s created by Maunsell for those lines that were less tolerant of the heavier 4-6-0 types. *MJS*

1994   **GROSMONT**

ailway preservation has come a very long way since those pioneering days back in 1951 when a group of enthusiasts formed a volunteer group to save and run the Talyllyn Railway, which became the first volunteer-run preserved line in the UK.

Only two narrow gauge preserved lines ran under British Railways ownership - the Welshpool & Llanfair Railway and the Vale of Rheidol. Therefore, since this volume concerns itself with the fall and rise of *British Railways* steam, these two lines are included in our review. The first provides us with an insight into those very early years of preservation - the Welshpool & Llanfair's last train under British Railways ownership ran on 3 November 1956.

Just four years later in 1960 a group of already active enthusiasts, no doubt encouraged by the progress being made by the fledgling Talyllyn's activities, formed the Welshpool & Llanfair Light Railway Preservation Company Limited. This enabled them to negotiate a lease on the line from British Railways and to start the mammoth task of clearing the track of several years of growth.

Progress at first was slow, as this was well before the advent of grants and considerable enthusiasm for steam nostalgia - after all, steam was still running throughout the country on main lines and branch lines! Despite the local council not

THE WELSHPOOL & LLANFAIR RAILWAY

Narrow gauge railways tend to be dismissed by many main-line enthusiasts, and 'The Little Trains of Wales' can be viewed as toys against their larger brethren. Two, however, have enjoyed service under the aegis of BR.

Above: The WLLR once had a direct connection to the main line at Welshpool, but sadly lost it after initial closure. Thus the current railway can only reach the outskirts of the town, but this has not prevented huge success in development and public appeal. The two ex-BR locos – Nos 822 *The Earl* and 823 *The Countess* – are seen here running into the station at the other end of the line at Llanfair Caereinion on 29 October 2006, the last day of the season and a celebration of 50 years since the 'last train' under BR, organised by the WLLR's 'West Midlands' group. *MJS*

Right: The top end of the VoR is at Devil's Bridge, and the location, popular with so many, provides stunning views and excellent walks from the station. In April 1968, still under BR operation – denoted by the 'double arrow' logo on the carriage sides and the blue loco and coaches – the three-coach train waits for its time of departure in bright spring sunshine. Note the catch point on the track on the left, leading into the dead-end siding. *MJS collection*

BRITISH RAILWAYS 2006 — **LLANFAIR CAEREINION**

THE VALE OF RHEIDOL RAILWAY

BRITISH RAILWAYS 1968 — **DEVIL'S BRIDGE**

allowing trains to run on the 'behind the houses' town section, effectively isolating the line from the main-line station and the trans-shipment sidings, the preservationists made good progress by moving the 'base camp' to Llanfair Caereinion and working back to a new Welshpool terminus at Raven Square. The line was purchased from British Rail for £8,000 in March 1974 - a lot of money at the time. It took until 1981 for services to be resumed to Welshpool, commencing on 18 July with, not surprisingly, considerable celebration.

The second of the narrow gauge lines, the Vale of Rheidol, has the unique distinction of actually running the last steam-hauled passenger service on British Railways! Although 1968 is the focus of much attention, this line between Aberystwyth and Devil's Bridge was owned and operated by British Railways/British Rail right through until 1989, when it was privatised. The railway is now owned and operated by a charitable trust.

Holidays have always played an important part in railway history. Before the advent of the mass ownership of motor cars, and cheap airline flights, the choice was clear – charabanc or train! The railways advertised their services directly and effectively to the would-be holidaymaker; indeed, they even provided accommodation in railway hotels or camping coaches.

Many of the seaside holiday destinations were to be found at the end of branch lines, which became increasingly costly to

THE WEST SOMERSET RAILWAY

Above left: Minehead often plays host to visiting large tender locomotives in addition to its own regular fleet. Here we see 'A4' Class 4-6-2 No 60019 *Bittern*. Note the corridor-fitted tender, a feature of some of these fine engines when first built in 1935, although not *Bittern*; it is a recent change enabling crew changes on longer runs. *Peter Rowlands*

Left: On the same Spring Gala day, 29 March 2009, LNER meets Southern on a GWR branch! 'West Country' Class 4-6-2 No 34046 *Braunton* joins No 60019 *Bittern* to await their next turn of duty. *Peter Rowlands*

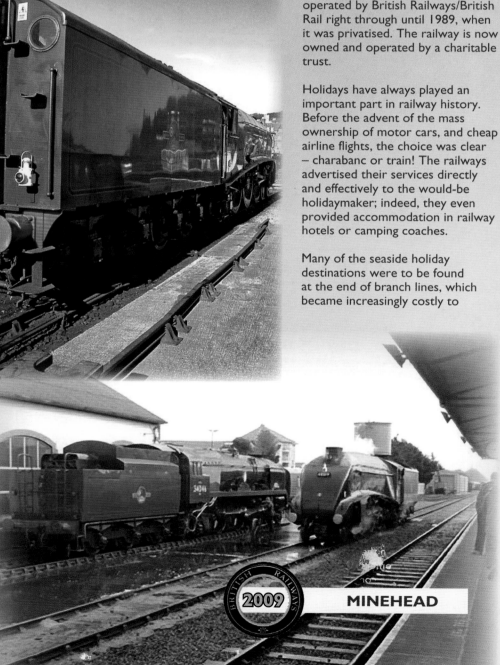

2009   MINEHEAD

run, particularly with traffic being of a seasonal nature. One of the longest branch lines ran between Taunton and Minehead. Although the presence of the Butlin's Holiday Camp helped keep this line open for years longer than many, it succumbed and closed under British Railways ownership in January 1971. Ironically this coincided with the start of the rapid growth in public interest and awareness of Britain's industrial heritage. Coupled with a growth in short breaks, supplementing the traditional week or fortnight away, the prospects for reopening the line as a heritage railway were potentially good. So it proved to be, and the West Somerset Railway reopened the line in 1976 and continued in stages until the route stretched from Minehead to a new station at Norton Fitzwarren, opened completely on 1 August 2009. A triangle is under construction, tantalisingly close to the main line, to enable the WSR to better accommodate incoming excursions via the main-line link.

Immaculate! As with the previous two views, the West Somerset Railway volunteers are to be commended on the superb polishing job carried out on all locomotives, home-based and visitors alike – your authors have witnessed their efforts on a regular basis! Here '4900' 'Hall' Class No 4936 *Kinlet Hall* stands at Minehead gently simmering away before taking the run up to Bishops Lydeard with an afternoon working during the Spring Gala in March 2009. *Peter Rowlands*

THE SEVERN VALLEY RAILWAY

2008   ARLEY

Looking over the bridge parapet at Arley towards Kidderminster, we see 2-6-2T 'Prairie' tank No 4566 approaching on a train for Bridgnorth. The semaphore signals on the SVR are among the finest examples to be found on preserved railways, and have indeed won awards.

First introduced by the GWR in 1906, the '4500' Class, of which No 4566 is a fine example, were a lighter-weight development of the slightly earlier Churchward '4400' design introduced in 1904. Classified 4MT, here the loco is fulfilling a role for which the class was originally designed - branch-line duties.

Inset right: Trapped behind bars! Seen through the metal of the station footbridge on 21 September 2008, No 4566 waits at Bridgnorth before beginning the early afternoon run to Kidderminster. *MJS*

2008   BRIDGNORTH

TODDINGTON

THE GLOUCESTERSHIRE WARWICKSHIRE RAILWAY

closure on 1 November 1976, following the derailment of a goods train. Lifting of the rails commenced in July 1979.

Starting without track is not the most auspicious start to an ambitious plan to reinstate a railway! The Gloucester Warwickshire Railway Society was formed in August 1976, close to three years before the track on the route was lifted. Although failing in their initial objective of keeping the line running under BR ownership, the Society proved to be made of stern stuff and was not to be thwarted!

The Society became the Gloucestershire Warwickshire Railway Trust in 1977, and the Gloucestershire Warwickshire Steam Railway Plc was formed in 1981 to preserve the line. The first public passenger trains ran on 700 yards of relaid track for the first time in 1983. In the following years the line has steadily grown and developed. The route is currently some 10½ miles in length and stretches from Toddington all the way to Cheltenham Racecourse. Stratford-upon-Avon and a national network connection still beckons and history tells us that this goal is certainly one that this group could well score!

Having already closed to passengers effectively from 3 January 1966, but seeing use for the very occasional special passenger service to Cheltenham Racecourse station between 1971 and 1976, the line from Cheltenham to Stratford-upon-Avon had survived for goods traffic and diversions until final

Above: In the bright and warm summer sunshine, No 34007 *Wadebridge* shows off the smooth, clean lines of its design as it accelerates away from Toddington station on 1 June 2007 with a six-coach load bound for Cheltenham Racecourse. Another Barry escapee, it arrived there in April 1966 after withdrawal from Salisbury the previous October and stayed until 1981. Moving to Cornwall, it was finally restored under the aegis of the Bodmin & Wenford Railway.

Right: The one major flaw in the heritage movement's attempts to recreate past scenarios is that, generally, the locomotives look far too clean. In this view, however, from 17 November 2007, ex-LNER 'J15' 0-6-0 No 65462 is suitably 'weathered' as it quite accurately reproduces a branch-line train, complete with period uniformed footplate staff, on the Defford Straight between Toddington and Winchcombe. *Both MJS*

DEFFORD STRAIGHT

Mince Pie Specials' was the theme for the ELR's customary Boxing Day timetable in 2008 - a festive treat of a complimentary mince pie for all passengers! On the last train of the day, No 45407 creates a wonderful spectacle in silhouette at Burrs, heading the 1446 service from Bury as the lowering sun catches the exhaust and falls through the tree to illuminate patches of the field in which the photographer is kneeling!

It is hardly surprising that the North of England, so rich in industrial skills and heritage, is home to many preserved lines, of which the East Lancashire Railway is a prime example. Reopened in part during 1987, following final closure by BR in 1980, the line now runs from Bury to Heywood via Ramsbottom and Rawtenstall. The ELR is run by a three-way partnership between the East Lancashire Railway Preservation Society, the East Lancashire Light Railway Company and the East Lancashire Railway Trust. Passenger numbers have steadily grown and now average 120,000 per year

THE EAST LANCS RAILWAY

Having control over much of what happens, our private railways can create some poignant moments, but not many are as momentous as this. During a night shoot on 19 February 2010 at the ELR Gala, history is made with what is understood to be the first occasion that Nos 70013 *Oliver Cromwell* and 44871 have steamed together since their appearances on 1T57, the 'Fifteen Guinea Special' on 11 August 1968. With a gap of 31½ years, the significance cannot be overstated! *Both Tom Pickles*

THE NENE VALLEY RAILWAY

The Nene Valley Railway promotes itself as Britain's International Railway - being extended by the preservationists to the Berne loading gauge. The reason for this interesting decision lay in the fact that by the time the Peterborough Railway Society (PRS) was in a position to seek locomotives to run on the fledgling line most of the remaining unsold or unreserved hulks were in the 'long term projects' category, having rusted and rotted beyond restoration to running order in a short time frame. Richard Hurlock a PRS member had approached the society to provide a home for his ex-Swedish Railways 2-6-4T Class S1 oil fired No 1928. This was the catalyst for the consideration that foreign rolling stock might provide a solution to the lack of suitable UK stock.

A notable exception to this was BR Derby built Class '5' 4-6-0 No 73050 which had been purchased by Reverend Richard Paten and delivered to Peterborough under its own power on the night of 11 September 1968 - a month after the end of standard gauge steam on BR metals. Richard donated the locomotive to Peterborough City Council in 1973, it having been named *City of Peterborough* by Cllr. Philip H. Turner, Mayor of Peterborough in August 1972. The City Council then leased the locomotive to the PRS.

The original line, of which the current Nene Valley Railway is a part, was closed in stages, firstly, in 1964, the Peterborough to Northampton passenger service ceased, followed by Peterborough to Rugby in 1966. This left a dwindling goods service. Complete closure by BR in 1972 seemingly was to see the end of the line's 127 year life. However, Peterborough Development Corporation purchased the line between Yarwell Junction and Longville in 1974 and leased it to the Peterborough Railway Society.

In the years since then the line has developed progressively, being first passed for passenger running on 24 May 1977, between Wansford and Orton Mere. The line now runs from a recently opened Yarwell Junction to Peterborough (Nene Valley), a short walk from the city centre..

BRITISH RAILWAYS 2010 — **WANSFORD**

Below: Simmering in front of Wansford box on a gloriously sunny 22 May 2010, the immaculate Class '5' 4-6-0 No 73050 *City of Peterborough* rests between turns.

Right: Driver Neil Purillant can relax in the knowledge that trainee fireman Jim Gosney has a healthy fire ready judging by the glow emanating from the firebox! *Both Dave Streatfield*

THE NORTH NORFOLK RAILWAY

2010   HOLT

THE MID NORFOLK RAILWAY

2009   THUXTON

Above: Now known as the North Norfolk Railway, it has also been affectionately entitled 'The Poppy Line'. Preserving steam in that part of East Anglia, 'N7' No 69621 is pictured with the restored LNER Quad-Art set of carriages at Holt station on 11 March 2010, the day that the NNR celebrated the arrival of the first main-line tour to cross the new link between Network Rail and the heritage line at Sheringham. At the other end of the train is GER N2 No 1744, which can be seen at the buffer stops. The crew are using temporary arrangements to water the 'N7', since No 70013 *Oliver Cromwell* was to follow the working into Holt. Built at Stratford in 1924 as an LNER 'N7' 0-6-2T, No 69621 is the sole survivor of a class once comprising 134 examples, and succumbed to progress at Stratford on 6 October 1962, after a career spent often switching between London and Nottingham. *Cliff Thomas*

Almost a year earlier than the image above, we find No 69621 still in Norfolk but this time awaiting the 'right away' at Thuxton on the Mid-Norfolk Railway on 25 April 2009. New ballast for the loop through the station awaits track. The team at the Mid-Norfolk are making excellent progress in restoring this route, which currently runs from Wymondham to Dereham but has plans in the longer term to reach Fakenham. The station at County School, which lies between Dereham and Fakenham, has already been restored and features a fascinating museum - well worth a visit even before the trains once more run to this location. The passenger service between Dereham and Wells, passing through County School, ceased in 1964 and services between Dereham and Wymondham followed in 1969. The MNR preservationists ran their first passenger services from Dereham to Yaxham in 1996 and onwards to Wymondham in 1999. *Richard Waterhouse*

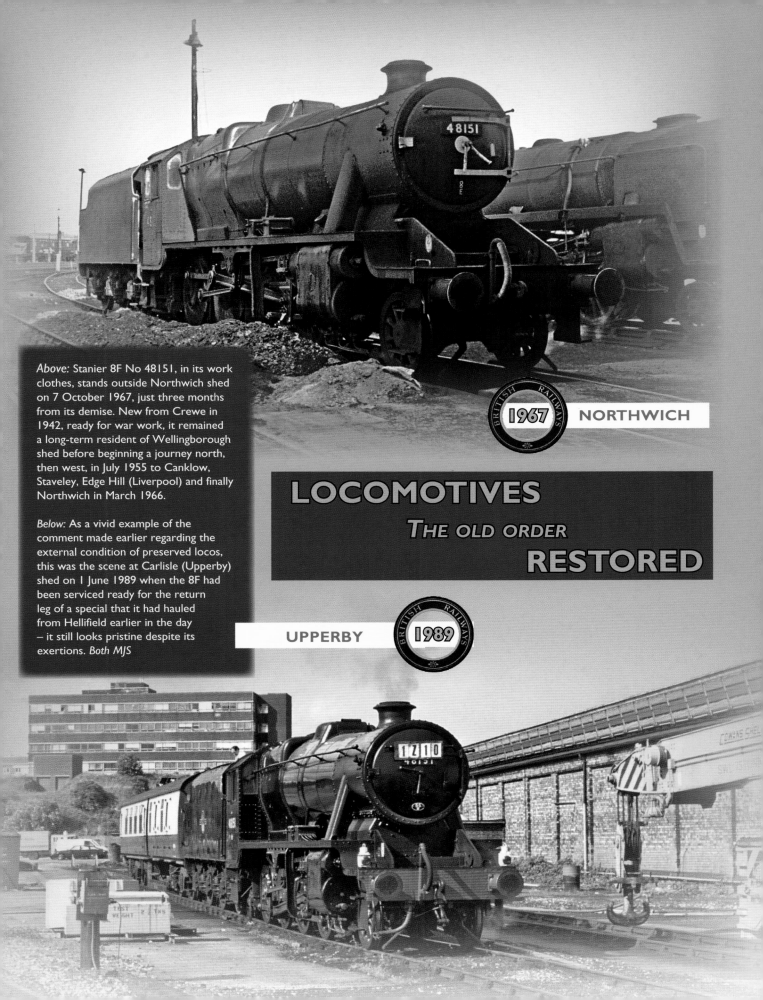

Above: Stanier 8F No 48151, in its work clothes, stands outside Northwich shed on 7 October 1967, just three months from its demise. New from Crewe in 1942, ready for war work, it remained a long-term resident of Wellingborough shed before beginning a journey north, then west, in July 1955 to Canklow, Staveley, Edge Hill (Liverpool) and finally Northwich in March 1966.

Below: As a vivid example of the comment made earlier regarding the external condition of preserved locos, this was the scene at Carlisle (Upperby) shed on 1 June 1989 when the 8F had been serviced ready for the return leg of a special that it had hauled from Hellifield earlier in the day – it still looks pristine despite its exertions. *Both MJS*

1967 BRITISH RAILWAYS **NORTHWICH**

LOCOMOTIVES
THE OLD ORDER
RESTORED

UPPERBY BRITISH RAILWAYS **1989**

c1962   WELLINGBOROUGH

Above: One of the most famous locos both before and after preservation is No 46100 *Royal Scot*. This view is undated, but is thought to be close to the end of the loco's working life in November 1962. It is understood to be waiting to restart its train at Wellingborough on its way from St Pancras to the north. For many years a celebrated traveller over the WCML, *Royal Scot* was 'brought down to earth' in November 1959 with a transfer to Nottingham shed and more humble duties. Despite its careworn appearance, it still proudly displays its full nameplate. *MJS collection*

2009   LLANGOLLEN

Left: That nameplate is seen in all its glory, trumpeting its North American tour of 1933 and its presence at the Chicago 'Century of Progress Exposition'. *Peter Townsend ?*

Bottom: Following preservation, many years were spent at Bressingham Steam Museum (see page 100), but after a protracted release earlier this century it has visited many locations, on and off the main line. On 18 April 2009, as LMS No 6100, it is seen at speed on the Llangollen Railway, heading for Carrog, in its garish LMS red livery but without the smoke deflectors that were so much part of its life. *Jack Boskett*

Is that a big end knocking? The driver of LSWR 'T9' No 120 shows concern as his charge approaches the then terminus of the Swanage Railway at Harman's Cross on 25 April 1992. The headcodes here refer to the presence on the train of the leading lights of the Middleton Press, who were celebrating the launch of their 100th book. Known as 'Greyhounds' for their speed over the Southern Railway, the 'T9s' served the railway well and several survived to Nationalisation. Two representatives continued until final disposal in 1961. Built at Nine Elms in 1899, No 120 had several homes over the last decade of its life, finishing at Eastleigh in November 1961, from where it was spared the ignominy of a visit to Barry by being adopted by the National Collection. *MJS*

1992   HARMANS CROSS

As we have seen in the preceding pages, with the demise of the steam-age railway in the years leading up to 1968 and that eventful day in August and the running of the 'Fifteen Guinea Special', the end was far from nigh!

However, time continues to march ever onwards and it is worth considering in this chapter, entitled 'Locomotives – the old order restored', the question as to whether or not these fine machines will be able to keep on being restored to running order. When your authors, together with hundreds of other enthusiasts, were making pilgrimages to the scrapyards of steam all those years ago, we not only witnessed the sadness of so many giants being slaughtered by the flames and intense heat of the cutter's torch. We also

No 7903 *Foremarke Hall* was privately restored to working condition at the Swindon & Cricklade Railway, but sadly the line at that time was not long enough for the loco to stretch its legs and it has thus spent much of the subsequent period on the Gloucestershire Warwickshire Railway. Seen storming out of the tunnel on the southern approach to Winchcombe station on 17 November 2007, it is moving empty stock from a race special to Cheltenham before it is needed again later that day. Completed at Swindon Works, but in BR days, its first home was Old Oak Common from 31 May 1949. It was a loyal servant there until a switch to South Wales saw it at Cardiff East Dock, from 2 November 1963 to 20 July 1964. It was then but a short trip to Barry, where it stayed until 1981. *MJS*

BRITISH RAILWAYS 2007

WINCHCOMBE

Top: The 'Coronations' – aka 'Duchesses' and/or 'Semis' (due to the retention by some of the sloping smokebox top after rebuilding from streamlining to standard design) – were the most powerful locomotives on the LMS system. Introduced by Stanier as an enlarged version of his 'Princess Royal' Class in 1937, a total of 38 were provided to haul the prestige expresses along 'The Premier Line' out of Euston. No 6233 *Duchess of Sutherland* was new from Crewe Works on 18 July 1938 and is seen here at Shrewsbury on one of its earliest running-in rosters. *MJS collection*

Centre: Not far short of 70 years later, the LMS livery is once again worn by No 6233, but also the smoke deflectors, which were such a part of the design, and the double chimney, fitted on 8 March 1941. It received its BR number on 29 September 1948 and pounded the beat over the WCML until dieselisation and electrification tolled the death knell at Edge Hill on 8 February 1964. Thankfully, Billy Butlin bought it for his camp at Ayr the following October. Its subsequent history is an interesting one, right up to being restored to the main line and even hauling Royalty! It is here entering Bewdley on 23 September 2006. *Horace Gamble*

Right: Sister loco No 46229 *Duchess of Hamilton* was another of the class rescued by Billy Butlin, at Minehead this time, that has since returned to the main line. On 4 May 1985 it coasts down Saunderton bank with the 'South Yorkshireman' special working. New in September 1938 it stood in for No 46220 *Coronation* at the New York World's Fair in 1939 and carried that false number between 20 December 1938 and 20 April 1943. It was fitted with a double chimney on 20 April 1943, had its streamlining removed on 10 January 1948, and was renumbered by BR as 46229 on 9 April of that year. *MJS*

1938   SHREWSBURY

2006   BEWDLEY

1985   SAUNDERTON

saw the evidence of seeds being sown for the future. At first there were just a few messages scrawled on cabs and boilers - 'RESERVED for ... Society', 'PLEASE DO NOT REMOVE PARTS...', 'PURCHASED by ...'. As the months and years passed the messages became more and more prevalent, in part because there were fewer and fewer complete locos left standing and the number to be saved therefore became far more evident. Just as a gardener knows that not all seeds go on to reach maturity, so it has proved to be with many of those early targets planned for restoration.

Looking back now, how sad it is that all of them could not have succeeded, so that the locomotive pool today could have been that much larger and stretch that bit further. Today's preserved lines are finding it increasingly difficult to source sufficient steam motive power to run the level of services that an ever-growing – thankfully – and enthusiastic public desires. A real dilemma could be building; on the one hand line lengths continue to grow and passenger numbers continue to rise, while on the other the availability of the steam power and indeed the 'old-fashioned' rolling stock that creates the atmosphere that fuels the growth is becoming

'Standard' Class 5 No 73096 is not the most frequent of visitors to the main line, and certainly not to Brunel's Paddington-Bristol 'racetrack'. On 28 March 2004 it storms away from Didcot at Denchworth with Steam Dreams' 'The Cathedrals Express', actually running a few minutes early. Originating at Alton at 0730, the train reached the ex-GWR main line via Feltham Junction before heading westwards for an arrival at Gloucester at 1310. Despite a prompt return departure at 1718, and being 9 minutes early at Kensington Olympia, 15 minutes were lost between Clapham Junction and Barnes, leading to an arrival 35 minutes late back at Alton, at 2323. New in December 1955, No 73096 served many sheds in both the Midland and Western regions before surrender at Patricroft on 2 December 1967 and a journey to Barry Docks. It was to be 1985 before it left, for preservation on the Mid Hants Railway and a final return to steam. *MJS*

2004   SHRIVENHAM

ever more stretched and ever more difficult to find and maintain.

Thus while the old order has indeed been restored - fine examples can be seen in these pages - it is time to look to the future!
Why?
Because if we are to continue to enjoy these wonderful machines, and to pass on to future generations the thrill and the real experience of 'travelling back in time' behind a steam locomotive, sitting on cushioned and sprung seats, in compartments that ooze the atmosphere and have

that distinctive, wafting, whiff of steam trailing back from the engine, action will be required and an even greater degree of coordinated planning will almost certainly be needed.

The degree of cooperation between preserved railways is already considerable, with locomotives and rolling stock being loaned and borrowed to supplement each other's requirements for special events and galas, etc. The National Collection based at the National Railway Museum at York also helps to supplement the available motive power. However, all these original locomotives are becoming increasingly difficult and costly to maintain

Since 1968, when BR initially introduced a 'steam ban' on the then steam-free network, there have been many rail tours and tour operators. All have aimed and achieved over time to bring steam operation back to the system, but while many have concentrated on the main routes, there have been those keen to investigate the more localised and/or branch lines. The ex-Cambrian route from Machynlleth to Porthmadog and Pwllheli was favoured on a number of occasions, giving passengers the delight of crossing the once-threatened Barmouth Bridge and experiencing the spectacular Cambrian coastline. On 27 August 2008 No 76079 draws the empty stock for 'The Pocket Rocket' from the siding at Machynlleth, in dismal weather conditions, ready to pick up its travellers, complete with West Coast Railways' 'The Cambrian' headboard and Welsh flags on the bufferbeam. Leaving on time at 1005, arrival at the Pwllheli terminus was 2 minutes ahead of schedule, at 1238; the return departure was equally on time, but sadly Machynlleth was reached some 24 minutes late, after an enforced 37-minute delay at Barmouth to wait for the passage of a service train. *MJS*

2008   **MACHYNLLETH**

HEY BRIDGE

as age takes its toll. Your authors support a view that is growing in momentum that it is time to consider pooling resources to establish a new build programme of say ten examples of a single loco class from the past. The European aerospace industry has shown how many different engineering facilities can each build various components that are eventually brought together to produce the finished article.

The choice of locomotive would need to be considered carefully but would need to be based on the suitability of the locomotive to carry out the most prevalent duty requirements of the majority of preserved lines - this would probably suggest a relatively powerful tank engine rather than a tender locomotive. Without doubt there will be no shortage of suggestions from the enthusiast fraternity as to which class, type and wheel arrangement should be chosen...

The preservation of locomotives and the maturity of the heritage movement has given opportunities for scenes that would never have been experienced under normal BR running. Designed for and exclusively used in Scotland, Gresley's 'K4s' were predominantly used on the West Highland route from Glasgow, with many hills to climb or circumvent. While the Severn Valley route is no mirror of that further north, No 3442 (BR No 61994) *The Great Marquess* makes a fine stab at evoking past operations on the single line at the upper end on 22 April 1989, as it passes over Hey Bridge on the approach to Eardington station. *Horace Gamble*

Main picture: The 'Britannias', being the first 'Standard' design to appear post-Nationalisation in 1948, caused a stir among the traditional railway fraternity with their new and bold ideas for design and maintenance practices. The final member of the 55-strong class to work on BR, No 70013 *Oliver Cromwell*, superbly demonstrates the new order, following preservation on the GCR, forming the mid-afternoon Loughborough-Leicester North service on 5 May 2008 and masquerading as one of the former crack expresses of the route.

Centre: The class leader, 1951-vintage No 70000 *Britannia*, was restored to main-line running on 27 July 1991 after many years in store, with the appropriately titled 'The Britannia Phoenix' rail tour from Crewe to Hereford and back. It is seen about to pass the level crossing on the outskirts of Leominster on the outward run.

Bottom: Caught 3½ years later, it is still gleaming but now within the confines of a heritage site. Semi-naked, without smoke deflectors, it stands in Didcot yard on 26 February 1995. *All MJS*

2008 BRITISH RAILWAYS — LOUGHBOROUGH

THE SOUTH YORKSHIREMAN
70013

1991 BRITISH RAILWAYS — LEOMINSTER

1995 BRITISH RAILWAYS — DIDCOT

70000

Your authors will, dear reader, for fear of favour or offence, decline to proffer a preference here!

Thankfully, over these many years of active preservation a number of excellent facilities have developed throughout the country where locomotive repair, restoration and overhaul is taking place on a daily basis. A considerable amount of time has been spent over all these years to bring locos back from the dead. The examples seen within these pages bear testament to that fact. The hard work, enthusiasm and commitment of all those who work at these locations deserves recognition and our considerable gratitude.

Restoration is, of course, a never-ending task. 'Roadworthiness' and safety are paramount, with regular minor and major overhauls required together with the mandatory renewing of boiler certificates every 10 years or so. The number of rotting hulks has been slowly but surely diminishing over the years, and this, coupled with the engineering expertise available, makes prospects for a multiple-loco new-build programme more likely.

Given that such a scheme could be realised, the availability of such new locos to carry out the day-to-day duties would still provide a desirable journey but also enable a reduction in mileage and therefore wear and tear on the more precious original locomotives. The appearance of originals in service would become an even greater attraction, as they would be seen in action that little bit less often.

There is no doubt that 'British Railways' steam is still very much alive and kicking, but if the wheels are to be kept turning the level of volunteers will need to be maintained and this is an important aspect in planning for the future. Volunteering on a preserved railway, while not for everyone, can be an enjoyable experience - a way of meeting new people, and learning new or developing existing skills. As Britain in recent decades has moved from being an economy built on manufacturing to more service-based, many of the heavy engineering and 'getting your hands dirty' jobs have disappeared. When steam was the predominant form of traction on Britain's railways the mindset and skills base were very different. Youngsters were raised in an environment of construction - *Meccano, Airfix, Revell, Frog* and many other construction kits emulated in miniature many of the items being built in full size. Apprenticeships played a greater part

From the earliest days, the railway has had need of smaller 'maid of all work' engines that could handle jobs in marshalling yards, local yards, local 'trip' workings and, in emergencies, give assistance on the main line. The LMS had more than 400 of the 3F 0-6-0T 'Jinty' design, introduced from 1924, which gave sterling service over many years right up to close to the end of steam on BR, the last five being withdrawn in 1967. No 47383 – LMS No 16466 – saw life in squadron service between emerging from Vulcan Works in 1926 and 7 October 1967, and was one of the last to be dispensed with. Serving masters from Chester to Carlisle after 1948, an initial withdrawal came at Newton Heath on the last day of 1966, but restatement came on the following 4 February together with a move away from the North West for a six-month reprieve at Westhouses in Derbyshire. It is seen relinquishing the single-line token at Bewdley on 22 April 1989, with its passengers bound for Kidderminster.
Horace Gamble

BRITISH RAILWAYS **1989**   **BEWDLEY**

in the way of life, and introduced young workers to jobs constructing the real thing. Not that such things have entirely disappeared, but the digital revolution has very much changed the way we live and work. Competition for leisure time has increased, with more TV channels, video and computer games, etc. Interestingly, model railways have continued to hold considerable fascination for young and old alike, being seemingly resilient to change; indeed, this 'age of the chip' has seen a considerable growth in interest in recent years. Just what effect such trends will have on the number of people willing to volunteer in the future only time will tell, but let us hope that the new age of steam will not only be maintained but will also be developed for future generations to enjoy!

The West Somerset Railway is another that has devoted time and great effort to carve its place in the Premier League of heritage railways, taking advantage of its seaside destination and its ambitions to reinstate the link to the main line. Here echoing the halcyon days of GWR double-heading over the Devon banks, on 25 March 2000 Nos 7828 *Odney Manor* and 5051 *Earl Bathurst* are bathed in glorious low, late-afternoon sunshine as they approach a red signal outside Williton station with a train from Bishops Lydeard. Both were escapees from Barry Docks – No 7828 in 1981 (after going there in 1966) and No 5051 in 1970 (1964) – and both were 'on holiday' on the WSR on this day. *MJS*

BRITISH RAILWAYS 2000   **WILLITON**

Race to the North? Not quite, but certainly a race in the south! During the 2000 'Steam on the Met' celebrations, two ex-LNER passenger locos battle it out on their way north at Pinner on 29 May. On the left, Gresley's 4P3F 4-6-0 'B12' No 61572, built in 1928, just has the edge over its more modern companion, Peppercorn's development of Thompson's 5P6F 2-6-0 'K1', No 62005, new in 1949. While two steam engines have occasionally been seen at locations on the same day since the end of steam in 1968, rarely have they been pitted side-by-side, and this was indeed a rare sight to behold. Both have six coaches behind them, but No 61572 has the advantage of ex-Metropolitan Railway loco No 12 *Sarah Siddons* on the rear! *MJS*

PINNER

1997 GREAT BEDWYN

Another locomotive that has been a rarity on the main lines, compared to many of its contemporaries, ex-SR 'S15' 4-6-0 No 828 enjoys the opportunity to stretch its legs as it passes Great Bedwyn, on the Berks & Hants route, with 'The Wiltshire Wanderer' rail tour from Clapham Junction to Eastleigh on 6 April 1997. Yet another potential victim of the acetylene torch at Barry, it was moved to South Wales in 1964, after withdrawal from Salisbury, its home for more than 15 years, on 27 January of that year. One of five 'S15s' rescued for preservation, this 1927 product of Eastleigh Works left Barry in 1981 and returned to Eastleigh for eventual restoration. *MJS*

This is what steam on the main line is all about, proving that the appeal has not diminished over time, despite the ever-declining number of those who remember it for real. At precisely 1224 on a dull and chilly spring Saturday, 19 April 2008, spectators on both platforms gather to watch or photograph No 60019 *Bittern* as it blasts through Ashchurch station, its approach having been announced by its glorious chime whistle. Kingfisher Railtours' 'The Severn Valley Phoenix' was a special from Kensington Olympia to Bridgnorth and return, to celebrate the return to normal running on the SVR after the disastrous flooding of the previous summer. *Bittern* took over from the diesel locomotive at Didcot and handled the tour both ways to and from Kidderminster. *MJS*

2008 ASHCHURCH

BRITISH RAILWAYS 2009 — ABBOTS RIPTON

BRITISH RAILWAYS 2008 — DARLINGTON

Above: Initially appearing in grey undercoat, as seen here at Darlington on 29 July 2008 for its first move under its own steam, and for subsequent testing runs, No 60163 *Tornado* was eventually painted into a pseudo-BR green livery, complete with the 'British Railways' legend on the tender. *David Porter*

Main picture: On 7 February 2009, a week after it hauled its first passenger trip on the main line, 'The Peppercorn Pioneer', from York to Newcastle and back on 31 January, *Tornado* blasts south past Abbots Ripton with the outward leg of 'The Talisman' York-King's Cross special. *Richard Wells*

Ideas for 'new builds' on our railways – the recreation of loco types that have disappeared – is not new. Schemes have been launched and ideas floated, only to quickly disappear from lack of interest, support, finance or forward thinking. Thus it seemed that the idea would remain just that – an idea – but *Tornado* has changed the rules and there are now, seemingly, a multitude of similar projects, all claiming value and/or uniqueness, and some further down a road to successful completion than others. Undoubtedly, with some, the initial fervour and media interest will fade into failure, and in listing and commenting on some of these below (in purely random order) your authors are in no way commenting on their odds of success or otherwise.

The movement of No 60163 *Tornado* under its own steam on 29 July 2008 at Darlington was truly a milestone in the spheres of railway preservation and restoration. Conceived and created under the auspices of the 'A1 Steam Locomotive Trust', it was unique in a number of ways. It was the first main-line steam locomotive built in this country since *Evening Star* in 1960; it was not attempting to recreate a pre-existing engine, but took the next consecutive number after the previous last of Peppercorn's 'A1' Class 4-6-2s; it was built to be capable of 100mph running; it was the first to initially feature its creator's website address on its tender; and was the first to feature in a 'race to the north' in a broadcast of BBC TV's Top Gear programme. In grey undercoat until testing was successfully completed, it was then painted in LNER 'Apple Green' before beginning a mammoth set of journeys throughout England, both on the main line and to private railways.

Main picture: On the previous page we saw No 60163 *Tornado* at Abbots Ripton. Viewed from the other side of the tracks and slightly further north on the East Coast Main Line, we see the same train at Fletton near Peterborough. Note that the locomotive has yet to be named. *Alex Hall*

4-6-0 'Patriot' No 45551 also enjoys a uniqueness, in that not only is it the sole headline ex-LMS type to be under construction at the time of writing

but it has been adopted by the Royal British Legion as the National Memorial engine. The project is based at the Llangollen Railway and aims to fill a gap in LMS locomotive history that will represent the link between the 'Royal Scot' and 'Jubilee' locomotives (and even the evolution from the 'Claughtons'). Launched in 2008, with a goal of completion by 2018, the centenary of the end of the First World War, the project has fired imagination and progress has been impressive, with the frames dedicated by the British Legion at a ceremony at Llangollen on 2 November 2009. Creation of the frames

was by Corus Steel, which also acted in this capacity for Tornado and No 82045 (see later).

Chairman of the Patriot Society is David Bradshaw, who is also a key member of Didcot's Great Western Society 'County' project. Another 'evolutionary link', No 1014 *County of Glamorgan* will recreate the ex-GWR 4-6-0 that was withdrawn from Swindon shed by BR in May 1964. The number has been dictated by the decision to use the name in recognition of the pivotal part in railway preservation played by Dai Woodham and his Barry scrapyard

2009   PETERBOROUGH

(see earlier in this volume) and the fact that Glamorganshire County Council donated the frames and boiler from part of their 'Barry 10' collection – from Nos 7927 *Willington Hall* and 48518 respectively. Launched in 2004, considerable progress has been made at Didcot over the past six years and the prospect of the finished product, the result of much design, ordering, cutting, welding, bolting, etc, together with a mock nameplate, continues to enthuse those who witness it 'in the flesh'.

Another beneficiary of the dismantling of the 'Barry 10' collection is No 6880

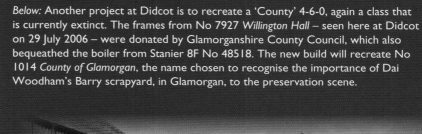

Below: Another project at Didcot is to recreate a 'County' 4-6-0, again a class that is currently extinct. The frames from No 7927 *Willington Hall* – seen here at Didcot on 29 July 2006 – were donated by Glamorganshire County Council, which also bequeathed the boiler from Stanier 8F No 48518. The new build will recreate No 1014 *County of Glamorgan*, the name chosen to recognise the importance of Dai Woodham's Barry scrapyard, in Glamorgan, to the preservation scene.

2006   **DIDCOT**

Below: A glimpse at the work progressing on the recreation of an ex-LMS 'Unrebuilt Patriot'. To be No 45551 and named *The Unknown Warrior,* the project has the support and endorsement of the Royal British Legion, and will become the new National Memorial engine. Having being cut earlier in the year, the frames are seen on shed at Llangollen on 8 November 2009, now complete with bufferbeam and beginning to assume the shape of a locomotive. On 4 May 2010 Vale of Glamorgan Council handed over a Fowler tender to the project, and this will be restored by Cambrian Transport Ltd. *All MJS*

2010   **LLANGOLLEN**

2000 DIDCOT

Betton Grange. Again assuming the next number to the final member of the original class, the 1998-launched project recognises that the 'Granges' were sadly missed, with none being preserved, unlike the various 'Halls', 'Castles', 'Manors' and 'Kings' that have survived. Being one of the earlier new build projects, progress has been slower than might have been hoped, but a boost was enjoyed early in 2010 when 'Hall' No 5952 *Cogan Hall* was acquired from Ken Ryder and was moved from Llynclys to Llangollen. A substantial amount of spare parts was also received. Although the plan is not to permanently rob 5952, various elements will save the 'Grange' recreation both time and money. The intention is to also fully restore 5952 in due course.

A 'Hall' that is being lost is No 4942 Maindy Hall, being used to 'back-create' No 2999 Lady of Legend – a representation of GWR's famed 'Saint' Class 4-6-0. A resident at Didcot since 1974, No 4942 is being transformed into its new guise by virtually reversing the step that the GWR took in 1924 of converting Saint Martin from its 'Saint' persona into No 4900, the first of a new 'Hall' Class. While the standardisation process undertaken by the GWR from its early days has made the recreation eminently possible, there have still been many detail differences that have tested the talents and skills of the engineers at Didcot. When completed, this new 'Saint' will close yet another gap in previously preserved loco types.

Above: As the first years of the 21st century progressed, 'new build' schemes seemed to become increasingly popular. Didcot Centre was heavily involved in this process, either directly or indirectly. The latter is more the case with No 4942 *Maindy Hall,* which was destined to disappear as an entity, donating parts to assist with the creation of No 2880 *Betton Grange,* under way at Llangollen, as well as being the main 'body' for the creation of a 'Saint' (see below). Its appearance at Didcot on 27 May 2000 would not seem to argue against this decision, its external condition at least militating against restoration as it stands. *MJS*

Below: You would be excused for thinking that this bears a striking resemblance to No 4942 above, and not without reason. In the attempt to create a new 'Saint' – a class extinct in 1953 with the withdrawal of No 2920 *Saint David* – Maindy Hall is being back-built to around 1913 condition, effectively undoing the transition from No 2925 *Saint Martin* to become the first 'Hall' in 1924! The larger wheels, deeper splashers, cab design and steps are all readily noticeable. With a temporary tender from the '6023 Project', what will become No 2999 *Lady of Legend* stands at Didcot on 18 November 2006. *MJS*

Space precludes exploration of further types, but your authors are aware of the Bluebell Railway's recreation of Beachy Head; a recreation of a 'B2/B17' 4-6-0, either in 'Footballer' or 'Sandringham' form; No 78059 to be converted to a tank engine as No 84030; creations of 'Standards' Nos 82045 and 'Clan' No 72010 *Hengist*; a new Holden 'F5' 2-4-2; and a new Worsdell 'G5' 0-4-4T. So, with restoration of yet more Barry wrecks, the steam fraternity is likely to be satisfied for many years to come!

2006 DIDCOT

The real test of whether the sight of steam on the main lines and the Herculean efforts to put it there are successful is the reaction and support of the public. Where and when Network Rail allows steam onto an already congested system, it is essential that the steam locomotive and the public coming to view it behave themselves! On certain occasions, privately organised charters are successful in claiming brief room on the tracks, such as BR 'Standard' 4MT 'Mogul' No 76001 (actually 76079 in disguise!) seen crossing the River Lochy at Fort William on a charter on 12 October 2008. The juxtaposition of loco, bridge, rolling hills, water and greenery, together with the smoke, creates a wonderful evocative of the magic of steam. *John Whitehouse*

2009

RIVER LOCHY

APPENDIX — A selection of locations to explore ex-British Railways STEAM

Railway / Centre	Web address
The Avon Valley Railway	www.avonvalleyrailway.org
The Battlefield Line	www.battlefield-line-railway.co.uk
The Bluebell Railway	www.bluebell-railway.co.uk
The Bo'ness & Kinneil Railway	www.srps.org.uk/railway
The Bodmin & Wenford Railway	www.bodminandwenfordrailway.co.uk
The Buckinghamshire Railway Centre	www.bucksrailcentre.org
The Caledonian Railway (Brechin)	www.caledonianrailway.com
The Chasewater Railway	www.chasewaterrailway.co.uk
The Chinnor & Princes Risborough Railway	www.chinnorrailway.co.uk
The Cholsey & Wallingford Railway	www.cholsey-wallingford-railway.com
The Churnet Valley Railway	www.churnet-valley-railway.co.uk
The Colne Valley Railway	www.colnevalleyrailway.co.uk
The Dart Valley Railway / South Devon Railway	www.southdevonrailway.org
The Dean Forest Railway	www.deanforestrailway.co.uk
The Didcot Railway Centre	www.didcotrailwaycentre.org.uk
The East Kent Railway	www.eastkentrailway.co.uk
The East Lancashire Railway	www.east-lancs-rly.co.uk
The East Somerset Railway	www.eastsomersetrailway.com
The Ecclesbourne Valley Railway	www.e-v-r.com
The Embsay & Bolton Abbey Steam Railway	www.embsayboltonabbeyrailway.org.uk
The Gloucestershire Warwickshire Railway	www.gwsr.com
The Great Central Railway	www.gcrailway.co.uk
The Great Central Railway (Nottingham)	www.gcrn.co.uk
The Gwili Steam Railway	www.gwili-railway.co.uk
The Isle of Wight Steam Railway	www.iwsteamrailway.co.uk
The Keighley & Worth Valley Railway	www.kwvr.co.uk
The Keith & Dufftown Railway	www.keith-dufftown-railway.co.uk
The Kent & East Sussex Railway	www.kesr.org.uk
The Lakeside & Haverthwaite Railway	www.lakesiderailway.co.uk
The Lavender Line	www.lavender-line.co.uk
The Lincolnshire Wolds Railway	www.lincolnshirewoldsrailway.co.uk
The Llangollen Railway	www.llangollen-railway.co.uk
The Mid Hants Railway (Watercress Line)	www.watercressline.co.uk
The Middleton Railway	www.middletonrailway.org.uk
The Midland Railway Centre	www.midlandrailwaycentre.co.uk

Railway / Centre	Web address
The Mid-Norfolk Railway	www.mnr.org.uk
The Nene Valley Railway	www.nvr.org.uk
The North Norfolk Railway (Poppy Line)	www.nnrailway.co.uk
The North Yorkshire Moors Railway	www.nymr.co.uk
The Northampton & Lamport Railway	www.nlr.org.uk
The Severn Valley Railway	www.svr.co.uk
The Spa Valley Railway	www.spavalleyrailway.co.uk
The Strathspey Railway	www.strathspeyrailway.com
The Swanage Railway	www.swanagerailway.co.uk
The Telford Steam railway	www.telfordsteamrailway.co.uk
The Weardale Railway	www.weardale-railway.org.uk
The West Somerset Railway	www.west-somerset-railway.co.uk

On 7 March 2010 one of Britain's finest railway photographers, Brian Morrison, celebrated his 80th birthday. Brian will need little or no introduction to the vast majority of railway enthusiasts, certainly not those who have been readers of his own railway books, magazine articles and contributed photographic credits in so many other publications over many years.

Brian was born way back in 1930 when the 'Big Four' still held sway on the railways. It was not, however, until 1951 that he sent his first pictures to the railway press. His very first railway photo was taken that year at Liverpool Street station with a camera purchased out of demob money received at the end of his National Service. Success was quick to follow, with The Railway Magazine of October 1951 carrying his first published image (of a diesel!). The Brian Morrison railway photographic collection now contains in excess of 170,000 images and continues to grow...

Both your authors wanted to conclude this volume on a special note, in the continuing story of steam on Britain's railways – there is much to celebrate and that, for us, includes ALL the many photographers of steam. Brian started taking railway photographs just short of 60 years ago and has captured on film the years leading up to the decline, and onwards through the fall and then the rise of British Railways steam. We owe a debt of gratitude to men like Brian because through their lens they have captured the images that have kept the dream alive! There can in our opinion be no better man than Brian to represent this group of special people.

We therefore asked Brian to select a representative picture and to pen a few words by way of a reflective summary of this look at The Fall & Rise of British Railways STEAM. This can be found on the final page.

We thought it was 'the end' in August 1968, and not even the wildest optimist would have bet on what we are so fortunate to enjoy into the 21st century. Sadly, for No 48390 – for that is the identity of this forlorn 8F and not 70036 *Boadicea*, or *Earl of Ducie*, nor yet the 'Patricroft Flyer'! – it was the end, and its departure from Patricroft shed after this day in the sun on 2 August was to the scrapyard, not preservation. *MJS*

1968 PATRICROFT

INDEX

'The Blue Belle' special from London Victoria to the Bluebell Railway and back ran on 15 September 1963 behind LSWR-liveried 'T9' Class 4-4-0 No 120 and Caledonian Railway 4-4-2 No 123; it is seen here near Balcombe on the return journey to the London terminus. Although the decade of the 1960s was notable for the demise of the steam locomotive in normal traffic in the United Kingdom, it was also the time when steam traction became much more than museum pieces, operating alongside both diesel and electric motive power on the main lines. The various works and shed scrap lines could not cope with the volume of steam withdrawals, and a mass of locomotives were bought by Barry scrapyard, where the numbers could not be immediately broken up for scrap, thus giving many the opportunity to bid for a withdrawn engine. Many were saved in this way and today are back in traffic on most preserved lines and on main-line charters. Amazingly, some 123 different classes have been preserved from the GWR, Southern, LMS and LNER and constituents, and in addition there are many others from BR 'Standard' varieties, industrial types and from abroad. And apart from the newly built 'A1' 'Pacific' Tornado, another 10 classes that were not preserved are now in course of construction, including a 'Saint', a 'Grange', a Brighton 'Atlantic', a 'Patriot' and a 'Clan'! *Brian Morrison*

The Fall & Rise of British Railways STEAM